A Minnesota Mom

In the Land of the Ancient Mother

VOLUME II
A Vision is Formed

PATRICIA CARLSON STENDAL

Copyright April 2009
Patricia C. Stendal
All Rights Reserved

Printed in Colombia
By Ransom Press International
Addresses are in back pages of book

Library of Congress Cataloging in Publication Data

Stendal, Patricia C. 1930-

A Minnesota Mom in the Land of the Ancient Mother
Volume II: A Vision is Formed

>1. Minnesota – 1930's, 1940's, and 1950's. 2. Romance – Married life. 3. Church involvement – Young people's group. 4. Colorado, Yellowstone, Texas, Wyoming. 5. US Corps of Engineers – Alaska Highway. 6. Pioneer Girls – Boys Brigade. 7. Overcoming Depression. 8. Gifts of the Spirit – Hearing God's voice. 9. Lives of influential missionaries. 10. Missionary Call. 11. Answers to children's prayers. 12. God's provision. 13. Marie Monsen. 14. Shantung revival.

ISBN 0-931221-57-9

Acknowledgements

Thanks to all who have helped me put this book together. A special thanks to Ruth Ann Irwin, Sharon Hewitt, Carol Andrews, and Kaleb Stendal, who read the manuscript in various stages and added corrections and suggestions. My daughter, Gloria, once again, was my right-hand person in assembling the book, scanning and placing pictures and giving advice.

Thanks to Osvaldo Lara for his cover design and other art work, and to Martha Cecilia Jaramillo Rincón for page design and work with the pictures. There are many others also who have encouraged me along the way.

Most of the writing of this volume was done in the years 1982 and early 1983 before our oldest son, Russell, was kidnapped in August, 1983. (The very act of writing about my early years brought a surprising psychological and spiritual healing to my innermost being. The fact that my history had been written down on paper brought an unexpected rest to my spirit. I needed no longer remember it; I could lay my burden of past experiences down.) After the kidnapping, my writing was put on the back burner for almost two decades.

In 2000, my granddaughter, Alethia, and I stayed for a period of time with the Del Buerge family in the Yukon of Canada. Alethia upgraded my computer skills, and the Buerge's encouraged me to continue my writing. I got started again. Now four more books are in various stages of preparation. My desire is that my personal pilgrimage might be of inspiration and help to others as we all travel on to the Celestial City.

The Carlson Family about 1942.

These pictures were hand colored by my mother.

Patty, Grandma Winburn and Dorothe.

Darrell, Dorothe, and Patty about 1940.

My parents, Richard (Dick) Carlson and
Eva Mae Winburn Carlson about 1978.

My sister,
Dorothe Burton,
inherited all the
artistic talent in
the Carlson family.

Dedication

To my parents
Richard H. Carlson
and
Eva Mae Winburn Carlson

This narrative was written in 1981, five years before my dogmatic, hot-headed father and my devout, loving mother ended their long lives on this earth in the same year, 1986. Through the process of writing, wounds have been healed and scars erased, which had been unintentionally inflicted during my early years. My mother's voice still sounds in my memory, "If you girls want to bring me flowers, give them to me now, don't bring them to my grave after I am gone, I won't be there: I will be with the Lord."

With the perspective of the 20 years
since my parents went to their Eternal Reward,
I can look back down the corridor of the years and
appreciate the firm basis of faith they built into my
early life and the sacrificial love that they showed in giving me
a secure home to grow up in, paying my college tuition, and
always being there for me, even when I was an adult
and had children of my own.

Mother and Dad, thank you for your faithfulness.

And to my sister
Dorothe Mae Carlson Burton
Who lived these early years with me,
And who now is one of my closest friends and confidants.
"Sisters are for Always."

Table of Contents

Acknowledgements 3

Dedication 7

Forward 11

Volume I

A Vision is Formed

Chapter 1 15
    A Little Princess

Chapter 2 25
    The Twig Is Bent

Chapter 3 37
    A Child by Faith

Chapter 4 43
    The Terror That Comes by Night

Chapter 5 51
    A Futile Repentance

Chapter 6 55
    Clouds of Turmoil

Chapter 7 59
    The Darkness Before Dawn

Chapter 8 65
    First Rays of Light

Chapter 9 73
   The Vision Dashed

Chapter 10 77
   College

Chapter 11 85
   Chad Stendal

Chapter 12 91
   On Trial

Chapter 13 97
   Enduring Hardness

Chapter 14 103
   Adversities

Chapter 15 111
   I Married Adventure

Chapter 16 125
   Playing With Fire

Chapter 17 145
   Up and Down

Chapter 18 153
   Agony and Victory

Chapter 19 163
   The Promised Land

Chapter 20 173
   My Sheep Hear My Voice

Chapter 21 179
   The Vision Grows

Chapter 22 185
    Katherine's Visit

Chapter 23 191
    A Delay and Russell's Prayer

Chapter 24 199
    Vacation Bible School

Chapter 25 203
    Majel Meyer

Chapter 26 209
    Old Cars and a Risky Trip

Chapter 27 217
    Colombia Calls

Chapter 28 225
    No Connections?

Chapter 29 229
    Ka-ga-ba

Chapter 30 231
    Money From an Unusual Source

Appendix: Marie Monsen 237
    Bibliography 265
    Afterward 266
    Books in this series written by
    Patricia Carlson Stendal 268
    Books written by the Stendal Family 269
    Ordering Books 273

Forward

"How did you folks happen to go to Colombia?"

I have been asked this question scores of times. Finding this to be an impossible question to answer in a few minutes in the back of a church or across a dinner table, I decided to tell the story step by step as it happened.

My previous book, *Minnesota Mom, Volume I – Beginnings*, lays a background of the Kogi tribe and culture in the mountains of northern Colombia. It also tells our family background up to the time of my birth.

I felt intimidated about sharing my early life with the general public until I read the book by C. S. Lewis, *Surprised by Joy*. The quote at the beginning of this volume gave me encouragement.

To understand the miracle that God worked in my life, you have to understand where I started from. I was a timid nervous child, fearful and psychologically disturbed, later a teenager lost in a dream world of my own making, and still later, a disillusioned wife with thoughts of suicide. Without the benefit of even an understanding person to help me, much less professional counsel, God met me and guided me through all the steps necessary to bring me into a victorious relationship with Him. To Him be the glory!

I knew that my mother had a vital relationship with the Lord. Because of that, I could not be satisfied with head knowledge, a superficial relationship that later my husband would call, "easy believism." In the years covered in this

Part Two: A Vision is Formed

present volume, 1930—1962, I knew nothing of the underlying theology of what I was experiencing. Later, my husband, Chad Stendal, would sift through all the theological errors of our present day and come up with an explanation. This can all be read in the last part of his book, *High Adventure in Colombia*.

Baby Patty in South Dakota.

Patty about 18 months in Atlantic City, New Jersey.

Patty at 2 1/2 in Portland, Oregon.

Volume II
A Vision is Formed

I have been emboldened to write of it (my early life), because I notice that a man seldom mentions what he had supposed to be his most idiosyncratic sensations without receiving from at least one (often more) of those present the reply, "What! Have you felt that too? I always thought I was the only one . . ." In the earlier chapters, the net has to be spread pretty wide in order that, when the explicitly spiritual crisis arrives, the reader may understand what sort of person my childhood and adolescence had made me . . . I never read an autobiography in which the parts devoted to the earlier years were not by far the most interesting.

C. S. Lewis in Surprised by Joy

My dad always said that my picture should be on the Cream of Wheat box, because I ate so much of it.

After so many childless years, my mother adored me.

A rare relaxed moment with my dad somewhere around my first birthday.

Chapter 1

A Little Princess

South Dakota, 1930

With the birth of Patricia Anne, Eva's joy knew no bounds. To her mind there had never been a child so wonderful as this one. The relatives in South Dakota were not so impressed, especially Eva's nieces who formerly had been her favorite children and who now felt displaced by this new arrival. They saw only a fussy baby with a bald head, big ears, and sad, gray-blue eyes. But Eva would not let her Patty Anne be treated as though she were a common, ordinary, run-of-the-mill child.

A pink satin-covered baby album, completely filled with tiny writing, tells of my first months and my mother's complete devotion. The same book tells of reoccurring ear infections, and states that I was almost always hungry until at four months Mother started me on Cream of Wheat which I eagerly consumed. Also, when I was four months old, Mother and I traveled by train to Seattle, and I became acquainted with my problematic daddy, Dick Carlson. At the time of my birth he was working for Westinghouse, installing elevators in sky-scrapers in large cities. He also was a street preacher and rescue mission worker.

Minnesota Mom in the Land of the Ancient Mother
Part Two: A Vision is Formed

Dick, a World War I veteran of the U.S. Navy, had lived a rough and tumble life in the bar rooms of Minneapolis until he was converted to Christianity by the witness of my mother, Eva, a country school teacher in the Dakotas. Their romance had started before Dick joined the navy, but during the war years, Eva became a Christian through contact with Russian-German immigrants in North Dakota, and because of this broke their engagement. The amazing story of their relationship and Dick's conversion is told in Volume I of this series, *The Beginnings.* Dick's disastrous behaviour during the birth and death of their first child had caused Eva to take refuge with her mother in South Dakota during her pregnancy with me.

Eva would "fight the tigers" for her baby.

One of the first nights we were in Seattle, Dick, bothered by my incessant crying, lost his temper and shouted at me. Frightened that he would harm me, Eva swung at him and struck him sharply in the eye. As Dick gazed at her in shocked surprise, Eva informed him that she would "fight the tigers" for her baby. Mortified, Dick went to work the next day with a black eye and must have decided to handle the baby situation with kid gloves rather than his usual rough manner, and there were no further incidents.

The loneliness and depression that had plagued Eva in Cincinnati never returned, and she devoted herself to me. I never felt like an ordinary child but identified more with adults. Grandma Winburn and Mother's friend, Lois Paddock, played important roles in my early childhood. One or the other almost always lived with us, as Mother was not very strong after that first childbirth experience in Cincinnati. Mother managed to maintain in my consciousness that I was not like other children. I was special! I belonged to her and to God. I must not use bad words. I must not get dirty. If my hands became soiled, I went running to have them washed, holding them as far from my body as possible. My blond hair must be carefully brushed the first thing every morning into the popular Shirley Temple style curls. I was always dressed in lovely, frilly, starched dresses of pink or blue. Many of them were hand embroidered or smocked by Mother or Grandma. On the rare occasions when I was taken out, I received many compliments which delighted Mother. My daddy was not home much, but I knew he was out working for us and serving God.

Mother carefully taught me about God and His Son, Jesus. After our nightly prayer, Mother and I went to bed at 8:00 p.m. holding hands until I fell asleep. Lois went along with all this and treated me much the same as Mother did, although she was a little more practical and earthy by nature. But Grandma Winburn, who had come west in a covered wagon, homesteaded in Dakota, and bore and raised nine children on the frontier — losing four of them before maturity — thought Mother's method of raising me was ridiculous. She later told me that I was only saved from an untimely death from too much attention and cleanliness by the birth of my sister, Dorothe, when I was just under three years old.

Grandma Winburn and me.

Part Two: A Vision is Formed

I get acquainted with my baby sister, Dorothe.

Dorothe's birth was a wonderful, spiritual experience for my mother and father. We were then living in Portland, Oregon, the beautiful city of roses. Mother found a wise woman doctor to attend her and explained what had happened in Cincinnati and how my dad had behaved. "Don't worry about him," said Dr. Graves, "I'll take care of him." And so she did. She had him scrubbed up and gowned and taken right into the delivery room, an unheard-of practice in 1933. Dick behaved himself and was delighted with darling Dorothe Mae, a beautiful baby with curling strawberry blond ringlets, and huge, bright blue eyes. "Gift of God" they aptly named her.

But for me Dorothe's birth was a bombshell that completely disrupted my safe little world, shattered my kingdom, and toppled me off my throne. Awakening one morning, I found only Grandma in the house. No one had prepared me for the arrival of this new member of the family, however Mother had come up with a plan that she thought would work. Grandma showed me a rubber baby doll in a little basket that had appeared on the sofa during the night. Beside the doll was a complete layette of beautiful, hand-sewn, tiny clothes. Mother thought I would be so delighted with this gift that I would play contentedly and not miss her. She couldn't have been more mistaken. I didn't care about the doll at all. I just wanted my mother. Grandma told me, as per her instructions, that just as this baby had come for me in the night, a baby had also come for my mother, only she had to go to the hospital to receive hers. I had a crying tantrum and demanded to be taken to the hospital to see my mother. (Lois always declared that I had a lot of my daddy, Dick, in me.) But Grandma insisted that only my father could take me to the hospital and that I would have to wait until he came home.

The day was very long. I stood on the sofa by the front window until late in the afternoon when I saw my daddy step off the bus at the corner. (Dad always used public transportation to and from his work, leaving the car at home for Eva's use.) Running to meet him, I told him I wanted to see my mother. Soon we were in the car on our way to the hospital. Standing on the front seat beside him, I suddenly turned to him demanding in a stern voice, "Why did you take my mother away from me?"

I don't remember any answer being given, but Dad was fond of repeating this question of mine in later years. I think he was rather intimidated by me in those days, tough, ex-sailor that he was. He had had no sisters and had developed no skills for dealing with women. He did not know quite what to make of the little princess that my mother had turned me into. Arriving at the hospital, he grabbed me in his arms and started up the steep stairs to the front lobby. A nurse in a white cap met us at the top and informed my father that children were not allowed in the hospital.

"This little girl needs to see her mother!" he roared, plunging through the lobby and down the corridor to the elevator like a football halfback breaking through the line. Once we reached the maternity floor, there was no more trouble, the nurses having been alerted to treat this potentially violent man with care. After helping my mother drink a malted milk and looking at my baby sister, I was told that it was time to go back to Grandma and that if I didn't cry, I could visit Mother again the next day. As Dad carried me off down the hall, tears were running down my face, but I was saying, "I won't cry! I won't cry!"

Grandma Winburn and I shovel snow together.

Eva took a long time getting her strength back, but because of her concern for me, she begged to come home. Knowing the situation, Dr. Graves released her from the hospital but sent a practical nurse, Mrs. Carlsborg, with her. To me, Mrs. Carlsborg was a villainous intruder into our home. I would not let her touch me but insisted that Mother get up out of bed and care for me herself. I warmed up to Grandma during this time, and to give Mother some rest she read to me by the hour. I soon knew the stories by memory, and if she skipped a word or sentence in the effort to finish the book sooner, I called her to task. I remember my third birthday as a happy day with colorful roses blooming around the yard, and majestic Mt. Hood towering above the city.

A week or so after my birthday, Mother and I boarded a train along with Grandma and Dorothe to return to South Dakota. Grandma had agreed to stay in Portland until the baby was born, and now she insisted on being returned to her own home. Mother was miserably ill the entire trip, and I almost wore Grandma out with trips back and forth to the observation car. I remember the beautiful Rockies in the freshness of spring, and the train coiling around the mountains and disappearing into tunnels. From our car we could often see the engine far ahead or the caboose far behind.

Stopping in South Dakota long enough to help Grandma get settled, we visited the relatives and then left for Minneapolis with Lois in her cute little red "coupe" with a rumble seat. Lois was younger than Mother by five or six years, short, dark-haired and independent. She had been a school teacher and loved little girls and cats but had little use for boys or dogs. (For a long time I thought all cats were female and all dogs were male.) Lois had always adored me from the moment of my birth. She had substituted for Dick, pacing in the corridor in Aberdeen, South Dakota while I was being born and felt a special bond with me, almost as though she were a third parent, but now her heart was completely captured by the angelic, placid Dorothe.

Lois Paddock and me.

In Minneapolis, we entered the Carlson family home at 508 Knox Avenue North where we were welcomed by Dick's only brother, Eddy, and his wife Malvina. My Grandma and Grandpa Carlson lived upstairs, and the huge carpenter astounded me by descending the wooden stairway with such force that the house shook. He muttered, "Hup! Hup! Hup!" with each step. I took one look at him and named him "Bee Pa" I felt that Big Pa suited him better than Grandpa, and "Bee Pa" he remained.

Part Two: A Vision is Formed

Grandma Carlson, Aunt Malvina,
me and my mother
at 508 Knox Avenue North.

His tiny wife, Ingrid Christina, had lost a leg to a gangrene infection and kept to herself upstairs suffering greatly with phantom pains in her missing limb. These grandparents were very Swedish having immigrated to Minneapolis from Sweden in their youth. My Uncle Eddy was a fireman and Auntie Mal, his wife, became one of my favorite relatives. She too was very Swedish and made excellent meals. Coffee time with sweet treats was a regular midmorning and mid afternoon custom in the Carlson home. I have happy memories of this time.

Grandpa Carlson "Bee Pa" and Uncle Eddy.

Bear and my dad.

One morning on his day off, Uncle Eddy whisked me away from my mother and took me to the firehouse to show me off to his firemen friends. On the way home he stopped at a saloon that he frequented, took me in and sat me up on the bar and bought me a vanilla ice cream cone. Mother was horrified when she found out, and she and Lois soon after moved us to an apartment on 26th and Garfield Avenue South. Since I didn't understand the significance of the saloon, somehow I always associated Mother's indignation with the vanilla ice cream cone. After that I was always careful to choose chocolate as she did on the rare occasions when we were offered ice cream cones. I wish I had gotten to know Grandpa and Grandma Carlson better. My contact with them was infrequent, mostly on holidays and other family gatherings. Both passed away within a few months of each other when I was seven.

Part Two: A Vision is Formed

Lois, Eva, Grandma Winburn and Patty at Yellowstone.

Dick, Eva, and Patty at one of the sea coasts.

My hand is dipped into one of the oceans.
A few months later, my other hand was dipped
in the other ocean when my dad's work took us to
the other side of the USA.

Chapter 2

The Twig Is Bent

Minneapolis, Minnesota, 1933

Dad soon joined us in Minneapolis. His job had been completed in Portland, and with unbelievable good fortune, his new assignment was the main Post Office building in downtown Minneapolis where he would install the Westinghouse elevators. His assignments usually lasted only a few months. When one job was finished, we would move to another large city. One of my early claims to fame was that before I was a year old, I had been coast to coast and had pictures to prove it. When we were living in Seattle, one of my hands was ceremonially dipped in the Pacific Ocean, and later in New Jersey, my other hand was dipped in the Atlantic. Due to Dad's skillful mechanical ability, our family felt little effect from the nationwide economic depression of the early 1930's. However Dad's real love was not his daytime employment, but his evening and weekend avocation of spreading the gospel.

While on the west coast, Dad had joined fellowship with several other street and rescue mission preachers. These men had white trucks that were lettered on all sides with Bible verses and outfitted with sound equipment. They were a splinter group of a Plymouth Brethren background, operating outside of the organized church. These men disapproved of all denominations and wanted to go back to the example of the Early Church as described in the New Testament. They felt that all the true believers in a certain area should meet together, regardless of denomination. They were skeptical of church buildings and preferred to meet in homes. They did not approve of a salaried pastorate, but wanted each Christian worker to be self-supporting. Their hero was the Apostle Paul, and they tried to duplicate his methods as much as possible.

Dad had never really felt comfortable with the theological stance of his Holiness Bible Institute. On the other hand, this dispensational theology, relying heavily on proof texts, appealed to his fine intellect. An anchor verse was II Timothy 2:15, which in the King James Version mentions *rightly dividing the word of truth*. Applying this verse, the Old Testament was divided out and left for the Jews, as were the four Gospels and the epistles of John, Peter and James. These were considered interesting for us to read, we were told, but not directly applicable to us who were now living in the "dispensation of the silence of God," according to the theology of Dad and his friends.

While we were living in the apartment on Garfield Avenue, Dad purchased a 1934 Dodge van and equipped it with a phonograph and microphone from which music and messages could be amplified through a huge horn on top. At full volume, it could be heard several miles away. We were to see little of Dad after that except for suppertime on weekdays, because evenings and weekends he was invariably out with the van, aptly christened "The Gospel Car."

Dad's first Gospel Car at the Minnesota State Fair. This car became a fixture at such public events for some thirty years at, which time it was replaced by a camper mounted on a truck.

As Dad toured the city and neighboring villages with the Gospel Car, Mother devoted herself completely to us girls. As I turned four and went toward five, she began to harbor desires for more stability than the elevator constructor job offered. She began to talk of buying a house and staying permanently in Minneapolis. Dad was horrified. He was happy with his work, which required frequent change of location and paid well, thus supporting the family and also his ministry with the Gospel Car. His friends with other Gospel Cars moved from large city to large city. They abhorred permanency. (Who ever heard of the Apostle Paul buying a home and settling down?)

Some fifty years later, as Dorothe and I cleaned out the family home, we found some of Dad's personal letters from

Patty and Dorothe 1934.

this period. Tears came to our eyes as we read how Dad tried to defend his actions to his friends whose opinion meant so much to him. They must have all been bachelors or widowers, as they didn't seem to understand the needs of a family. He built a case for a man with a wife and children and an established location from the example of Philemon in the New Testament, but there was no evidence that his friends accepted any of his arguments.

Dad also had an extreme aversion to going into debt and an unrealistically low estimation of his earning power. He was sure that he would never be able to pay for a house. From the beginning of their marriage he had divided his paycheck equally with Eva, her share going for the household expenses — food, utilities, clothing, etc. His half went for the large items, taxes, insurance, and probably rent. What was left of his share was used to finance the Gospel Car ministry, treat his coworkers to coffee etc., and much found its way into the pockets of the needy souls who crossed his path every day, usually accompanied by a stern admonition to be more industrious and responsible. Offerings were not received in his meetings, and offers of financial help were firmly refused, except in the case of a very few trusted and valued friends.

Dad knew that the purchase of a house would have to come from his share of the paycheck, and it frightened him terribly. Nevertheless, Mother combed the south end of Minneapolis with a real estate lady, and eventually her dream bungalow was discovered at 4440 Bryant Avenue South. This house, our family home for the next forty-five years, was paid for in three payments at intervals of two months. This was so easy that Mother wanted to go right ahead and purchase rental property, but Dad would not be pushed any further. In later years he was to regret bitterly that he had not allowed Mother to proceed with her plans.

At this time Dad was faced with another important decision. The job of installing the elevators in the Minneapolis Post Office building was coming to an end. Mother had already insisted with the purchase of the house that she was not going to travel from coast to coast, changing me from school to school. Dad was offered a permanent job with the Post Office as the elevator mechanic to service the elevators. This was quite a step down for Dad, in personal prestige and satisfaction, as well as in pay, but he took the job. A plus for him was that by working alternate Saturdays, he could free up the next Friday and have a three day weekend every other week to travel with the Gospel Car. This was especially important as a new city ordinance prohibited sound trucks and street preaching within the city of Minneapolis. Now he and his friends could take

Patty in front of our new house in Minneapolis.

Part Two: A Vision is Formed

their ministry out of the St. Paul - Minneapolis area to the outlying communities.

As my fifth birthday approached, and the prospect of kindergarten loomed on my horizon, I announced that I would prefer starting in college and working down to kindergarten. Since I could gain no support for my ideas, I had to submit and go to kindergarten. The first day of school, I walked into the classroom and questioned loudly, "Where are the books?"

Seeing my disappointment at the few picture books she showed me, the teacher explained that we would learn to play this year and learn to read next year in first grade. I felt like I already knew how to play, but since my mother was standing between me and the door, I took my place with the other children mumbling, "I guess I can stand it for one year."

At home I kept taking books to my mother or Lois, who was back with us again after spending some time out on the west coast. I would point out a word, ask what it said, then thumb through the book finding other repetitions of that word. Soon my reading vocabulary was quite large. Lois soon took note of my interest and got out her Dick and Jane primers. I was on my way. Lois also taught me to write and do simple addition and subtraction. Later on Grandma Winburn got into the act and taught me the multiplication tables. I was like a sponge. I wanted to learn everything I could. I wanted to grow up and be treated like a big person instead of a kid.

In the first few days of being in our new home, Mother oriented us to the rules that were to govern this next phase of our lives. We were not to step foot off our own property in the backyard. In the front, we were not to go into the street, nor the neighbors' front yards, but we were allowed to ride our tricycles and later bicycles up and down the front sidewalk. Later we could go all the way around the block and eventually even to the park at Lake Harriet, which was several blocks away. We didn't worry about violence or kidnappings in those days. The only dangers were making a neighbor angry or being hit by a car.

Most of our neighbors were elderly couples, and we had very few playmates until a family with twin girls between Dorothe and me in age moved into the house next door. Even so, I had to have permission to go into their yard. We were not allowed to speak to strangers, accept candy or other treats, or enjoy Popsicles or soda pop as our neighbors did. (Mother made homemade root beer for us once each summer and doled it out sparingly as a special treat

Dorothe and Patty 1935.

as long as it lasted.) Above all, we were not to play with or even speak to boys. Luckily for my mother there were none around, only one tomboyish girl who lived at the end of the block and liked to dress in boys' clothes (blue jeans). As I approached my sixth birthday, I began to wonder about boys, the ones I saw at kindergarten. They certainly seemed colorless and uninteresting with their short haircuts and dark corduroy knickers. Lois said they were no good, that they used bad words and made a lot of noise. I certainly was glad that Dorothe and I were girls with long blonde curls and colorful dresses. The vague answer given by Mother to my question, "How does one tell if a baby is a boy or a girl before the hair grows in?" left me confused. Sometimes I woke up in the night wondering if someone had made a mistake in identifying my sex when I was born. My pictures showed that I had been such a bald baby. Would I someday have to cut off my golden curls and wear those drab boys' clothes? The very thought sent a shudder down my spine. I certainly hoped not.

My uneasiness around boys during this time must have been apparent. Two male classmates who lived in my direction took delight in chasing me home every day. Terrified, I ran as fast as I could, the boys right behind me, until they turned off a block before my house. My mother called their mothers to complain, but the harassment continued. They plagued me all during kindergarten. One afternoon near the beginning of first grade, I started home heavily laden with a school bag of books in one hand and a paper bag of science displays in the other. I no sooner left the school grounds than the two boys came at me again. Something kind of snapped in my head. I was tired of running from these bothersome boys. I suddenly turned around and went for them with the fury of a lion, hitting them with the books and sack and kicking their shins with my sturdy oxfords. My attack took them by such surprise that they failed to retaliate. Then I turned and walked stately and serenely down the block. Soon I heard the boys behind me, but they were also walking slowly. "We really should be good to girls," I heard one say to the other. "They grow up to be our mothers."

Another traumatic situation for me occurred when I was in first grade. After teaching us sight words with flash cards for several weeks, Miss Merriam, my elderly teacher, decided to pass out the primers and see if we could recognize words. In fact she told us to start at the beginning and see how far we could read. We were instructed to raise our hands when we came to a word we didn't know. (The teaching approach was entirely the memorization of sight words. We were taught no phonics or sounds until second grade.) To my surprise and delight, it was the same Dick and Jane book that I had read at home the year before. Near the end of the book I found a word I didn't remember, so I raised my hand. Miss

Merriam thought I had lost the place, so she turned me to the front of the book and told me to start again. "But I already read all that," I explained. "You couldn't possibly have," she scolded, "Start over again."

When I came home at noon, my mother heard my screams a block away. I had been terribly insulted and humiliated! My word had been doubted! I was not going to return to school! Since the afternoon session did not include reading, I returned; however the next morning I flatly refused to go to school. Mother tried everything; even involving my father, but I would not be convinced. I was not going to go to school anymore. Dad had to go to work leaving the problem unsolved.

Former teacher, Lois, stepped into the picture. I was stuffed into my jacket and dragged off in the direction of the schoolhouse, my heels scraping on the cement sidewalk as Lois pulled me along. Approaching the school, I realized that I was going to lose the battle. I started screaming that I was sick and felt like throwing up. Into the school building and up the stairs Lois dragged me with a grip of iron. Into the girls' restroom we went. Putting her hand on the back of my neck, she shoved my head within three inches of the toilet and commanded, "Throw up!" I did not!

She took me to my classroom where Miss Merriam now seemed like my best friend in the world. "What is wrong with my little Patricia," she crooned, enfolding me in her motherly arms. I sobbed on her shoulder while Lois beat a hasty retreat. Unbeknownst to me, Mother had called the teacher. Soon my desk was carried to the other side of the classroom where the 1A's were grouped. These children were in the second half of first grade because of fall birthdays. They had started the previous January. I was given a book that was much more challenging than Dick and Jane. This was a much smaller group, and now I would be with them as long as I was in the public school system. I was well able to handle reading and arithmetic, but my penmanship and spelling never quite caught up and were atrocious for years.

When my mother went to school for the regular conference with the teacher, the only problem reported was that I did not participate in group discussions. When Mother questioned me about it, my reply was, "I don't want to tell **them** all I know." This statement was illustrative of the "we versus them" feeling that had been instilled in me. My mother had effectively communicated to me that my parents, Dorothe and I formed the nucleus of a comfortable "in-group." We were right with God, knew the truth and were separated from worldliness. Lois, Auntie Mal, and Grandma Winburn were satellites to our nucleus. They were **almost** right, but each one had a few problems. All others were to some degree suspect. From conversation at the dinner table, I discerned that teachers and the neighbors were especially suspect. I could gain points at the dinner table with my father by recounting anecdotes from school that reinforced his suspicion of teachers. My father and his friends were fanatically anti-Catholic. I actually sized up the few Catholic children in my grade and wondered how I would do in hand-to-hand combat in the street with them. From hearing my father talk, I expected that it would actually come to that one day. In Dad's mind Lutherans and Anglicans were just slightly better. Had Dad not been raised and confirmed a Lutheran and failed to understand the way of salvation? Baptists, including Auntie Mal, were almost all right. Others fit in somewhere between.

The important distinguishing characteristics of our "in-group" were that we did not participate in moviegoing, dancing (defined by Mother as jumping up and down on first one foot and then the other, slightly different from jumping and skipping which were allowable activities), playing cards, lotteries, drinking, smoking, listening to the radio except for approved Christian programs or the news (Grandma failed this one with her soap operas), reading secular magazines except for *Time* which Dad liked, reading novels or fiction books (I failed this one, secretively reading under the bed, or in the bathroom, or on the neighbor's porch), or attending symphony concerts, circuses, or the like.

For some reason, I had actually been taken to the Barnum and Bailey circus the summer that I was four. Standing in line to buy the tickets, already weary with the dust, heat, and strange odors, I had turned to Mother and commented, "We don't really belong here, do we?" At least that was how Mother always told it. Of course we went right home, and that was as close as I got to the circus for many years. Mother was greatly mortified that God had had to speak to her through the mouth of a babe.

There were other customs for the women of our group. I believe they were based on the rules at the Bible Institute that Dad attended, and probably from the customs of the Russian-German immigrants that Mother idealized. Our hair must not be cut. No lipstick or red nail polish was allowed. Slacks could be worn only if sufficiently baggy for very special occasions like fishing in the north woods. Long stockings were required and should not be of a flesh color. Most of these customs were broken by Lois which made her suspect of not being a real member of our "in-group" at all. Mother took pity on Dorothe and me in the hot summer and let us wear ankle socks, but we always got a good bawling out from Dad the day we shed our long stockings. At least Mother let us wear brown or tan instead of the black stockings required by Dad's Bible Institute. Of course, no sleeveless blouses, tight sweaters, or low necklines were allowed. There were probably more rules that I have forgotten. Above all, boy-girl relationships were sternly frowned upon. I used to wonder how my dad and mother ever happened to get married, since it was so wicked to have a boyfriend or a girlfriend. No one ever gave me a very good answer.

Sometime when I was around four or five, I started developing unreasonable fears. I was taken to visit a farm, and I was terrified of the farm animals, even the baby kittens. Included in the phobia that I was developing were doctors, Santa Claus, wide open spaces, such as pictures of the sea, and the worst and most long lasting of all — any kind of fish. Each one of these phobias got their start in an unpleasant experience. For example, I developed an intense case of impetigo (sores on the face) when I was four, and a doctor painted my face purple with genitian violet, the standard treatment for that day before antibiotics. I felt utterly compromised and humiliated, so much for trusting doctors. A fishing trip with my cousins from South Dakota started the fish phobia. We hit a nest of sunfish, and they let me catch the first one. I was utterly unprepared for the flopping fish when they told me to pull in my drop line. They then started pulling them in, right and left, and letting the caught ones flop all over the bottom of the boat. I screamed out of my mind, completely hysterical, until my mother persuaded them to leave the best fishing of their lives and take me to shore. This phobia became an ongoing problem because every summer my family took a fishing vacation at the lakes in northern Minnesota. If forced to go out in a boat with them, I prayed with all my heart that they wouldn't catch anything, and they rarely did. My family did have enough respect for me to keep any fish they caught on a stringer on the outside of the boat.

Chapter 3

A Child by Faith

One of the mysteries of life was soon to be solved for me. At forty years of age, Eva found herself pregnant again. She was less than thrilled as her previous pregnancies and labors had been extremely difficult. From my earliest memories Mother had not been very strong. Housework was done in the morning hours, and after lunch we rested, visited friends or relatives, went on picnics or to the beach. Mother would say as she rested on the sofa in the late afternoon, "I have to save a little strength for getting supper." After supper we still maintained the 8:00 bedtime. All of a sudden, even I noticed that my mother was working harder than ever before, redecorating the house, and filling the basement with a record number of jars of home canned fruits and vegetables. What had happened?

Mother in her desperation, wondering how she would ever get through this pregnancy, took literally the verse in I Timothy 2:15 that says, . . .*Notwithstanding, she shall be saved in childbearing.* Theologians debate the meaning of the word "saved" in this context, but to Eva it was very clear. It meant that she would be saved from the anguish she had suffered in carrying and giving birth to her other children. She decided to take this entire experience by faith. She was never before nor after so full of vigor and vitality as during this pregnancy.

Part Two: A Vision is Formed

The day before Easter Sunday, 1937, I once again awakened to a house without Mother. This time there was no sense of desolation. We had been well prepared. Four-year-old Dorothe and I waited happily with Grandma until Daddy came home to tell us that we had a baby brother. Our joy was overwhelming. Dorothe and I sat on the front step of 4440 all morning, shouting in unison to every passer by, "We have a little baby brother!"

Although not quite seven, I suddenly knew how much I had missed the male influence in my life. I now envisioned this newest member of the family as being an active, noisy little boy, like my school mates to whom I rarely, if ever, spoke, running through the house, slamming doors, two or three friends trailing behind him.

Dick was elated. He had recommended to Eva a fine Christian doctor in whom he had total confidence and had caused no scenes at the hospital, although he had not been allowed into the delivery room. After much debate, they named the baby Darrell Winburn Carlson. One glimpse of baby Darrell in his bath relieved my mind once and for all of a nagging anxiety. No, I had not been mistakenly identified. I definitely was not a boy.

Mother had had an unusual experience during Darrell's birth. While in the delivery room, she had been put into a panic by overhearing the doctor comment to his staff that the baby's head was very large and most likely would not pass through the birth canal. (Antibiotics were still some years in the future, and caesarean sections were still rarely used.) In her fright Eva felt the Lord saying to her, "*aren't you taking this baby by faith?*" She immediately relaxed saying, "Yes, I'll trust you, Lord." At once she felt herself transported to a heavenly realm where she saw and heard things for which she had no words to communicate. When she became aware once more of the delivery room, she was praising God, and the baby had been born.

The hospital staff was impressed and one young intern came to her room later to question her. "What happened there in the delivery room?" he asked her. "I have heard many women curse God in labor, but I have never heard anyone praise God before." Eva felt that when she returned from the hospital to tell of her experience, many people would turn to God after hearing this testimony. However she found that when she tried to explain what she had seen and heard, she could only weep. Most people thought her experience had just been induced by an anesthetic, although the doctor maintained that no anesthetic had been used.

To Mother and Dad, the crown prince of our family had now been born. About the same time, Lois brought us a paper doll book featuring the English princesses, Elizabeth and Margaret, who were just a bit older than Dorothe and me. Dad never tired of explaining to me that should the royal family have a son as ours had just had, Princess Elizabeth would never be a reigning queen, but the rights to the throne would pass to the male heir. I did not at all resent my baby brother, but it was my first hint that there was something inferior about being born a girl. Up to this point I had felt that I had the best of the deal. My mother's life certainly seemed a lot more fun and interesting than my father's. However now I started looking at the boys in my class at school with new interest. If they were more deserving of the throne than girls, how was it that we girls outsmarted them in every subject? There were four of us girls who competed for top grades, and only one of the boys ever even figured in the competition. In contrast, the duller members of the class were all boys except for one girl. I vowed to make sure that the man I married was at least intelligent.

Up to this point my Christian training had been mostly in the hands of my mother. I had heard her recount her conversion experience among the strange people who did not speak English. Sometimes she would sing us a hymn in the German language used by these people. She also told us our father's testimony and exhorted us to never marry a man who wasn't a committed Christian. She often ended by saying, "It is a good thing I waited until your father was converted. I have hardly been able to live with him as it is, and no one could ever have lived with him like he was before."

She also made it plain that the happiest time of her life was in her twenties before she got married. She rode horses, had her own car, went camping with her girlfriends, and enjoyed the country life where she knew everyone in the community.

I was actually terrified of my father. His explosive outbursts were frightening, especially when directed towards Dorothe or me. His spankings, however, were not very painful. He used his razor strap or a rolled up newspaper; both of them made a lot of noise and inflicted little pain. On the other hand Mother switched our bare legs with a long stick freshly picked from the lilac bush right outside the kitchen door. That really hurt and could even leave red welts. I soon learned that my father could only spank us when angry, so I used a few delaying tactics such as a few minutes of dodging him around our oval dining room table. That usually dissipated his rage enough so I only got scolded. If he did get hold of me and started to apply the razor strap, I danced and cried as though he were killing me. The raging lion was actually a kind-hearted kitten, and he would quickly decide the punishment was enough. However sweet little Dorothe got lots more spankings than I did. When she was quite small, I would hold her tightly on my lap and make them spank me first, however later I thought she deserved more than she got. Her reaction to punishment was the opposite of mine. She would become quite stoic and defy them to hurt her. The more she acted like it didn't hurt, the harder

Our neighborhood play group in summer. (Patty with the inner tube, and Dorothe with the elephant bathing suit.)

Our play group in winter. Patty is in center front with the big, black boots; Dorothe is seated on the snow fort to Patty's right.

they spanked her. I never could see the rationale behind her course of action. Actually, we were not spanked very often, and when we were, it was usually for some accident like overturning our milk glass at the table. I believe Mother spanked us for disobedience or quarreling, but it didn't happen very often. My naughtiness was under cover, and mostly in my own heart.

Though they were infrequent, I felt that these punishments were unjust, and harbored resentment in my heart, especially towards my father. I knew that the punishments were not intended to be rehabilitative or even punitive, nor geared to the seriousness of the offense. They were entirely related to Dad's quick temper and personal irritation. Years later, I found Dad a magazine article that counseled against spanking children in anger. After reading it, Dad wondered aloud how else they could be spanked. To him, it would take a heartless monster to strike children without being angry.

I soon noticed that my parents dissipated their strict ideas of child raising on me. They were more flexible with Dorothe, and as we grew older some of the more severe restrictions were relaxed. When this happened, the rule was changed for both of us girls at the same time, even though she was three years younger. This rankled me quite a bit. Moreover it seemed very strange that our super-strict mother became quite permissive with her baby son, Darrell. Everything he did was cute in her eyes.

Dorothe, Lois, Darrell, our cousin Darlys, and me.

Chapter 4

The Terror That Comes by Night

My father started to take more interest in me when I was about seven. He taught me the books of the Bible in order and then assigned selected verses to be memorized. Lois started selling books, and one of the volumes she sold was *Hurlbert's Story of the Bible.* She gave us a copy for Christmas, and Mother made a number of attempts at a daily Bible story time for Dorothe and me. Somehow we never got very far, and every time she decided to resume the evening Bible story time, she started at the beginning, so we became very familiar with Adam and Eve and the Garden of Eden. For each story there was a page of multiple-choice questions at the back of the book, and I was always very happy when Mother asked us the questions, as I always knew all the answers. After we had learned all of Dad's favorite Bible verses, he offered us a nickel for every verse we memorized on our own. Mother directed me to the first chapter of John, and I earned quite a few nickels.

Sometime when I was around eight, I started bringing fiction books home from school to read. The first time this came to Dad's attention, I received a good scolding for reading lies. However I was rapidly becoming a bookworm, so I decided I could avoid Dad's wrath by reading only *Hurlbert's Story of the Bible* when he was at home. I really got into it and read it through five times by the time I was twelve. It was quite complete, including all the stories that were considered fit for children from Genesis to Revelation. Sometimes I read a chapter to Dorothe and then quizzed her on the questions.

At the dinner table, Dad always prayed first in his gruff, loud bass voice. I prayed next, then Dorothe, and soon Darrell was also able to say a simple prayer. When the relatives came to dinner, they complained that the food got cold while we all prayed. Dorothe and I were convinced that Dad thought that his prayer was the only one that got through the ceiling.

We started having devotional times when we gathered in the living room, and my father expounded from the Bible to us and taught us some more Bible verses. These sessions always ended by us all getting down on our knees and praying in order of age from the oldest to the youngest as did the German family in North Dakota so many years ago. My parent's prayers were lengthy and earnest, pouring out their hearts for unsaved relatives, especially Uncle Eddy and my mother's brothers. Dorothe's and my prayers were mostly asking God to bless as many relatives as we could remember.

Once in awhile one of our parents took us to Sunday School but very irregularly and to different churches. I was always terrified that no one would come to pick me up at the end of the session. This fear of abandonment was completely irrational, as I can't imagine a more over-protective mother than Eva. I vainly tried to memorize each turn the car made as we were driven to each new Sunday School. I firmly believed I might have to find my way home alone.

A change took place in our family customs when I was eight. One of my father's friends started a small church about a mile from our home, and Dad decided that our family would attend. We became one of six families and several single Bible Institute students that participated in the little church. It was just one step above the house meetings. There was no formal membership, and the doctrine taught there was for the most part compatible with my dad's beliefs. Since becoming stationary in Minneapolis, he was distanced from his former mentors with their Gospel Cars. However his own belief system had solidified by this time, and he was very rigid in his opinions, making doctrinal agreement a requirement for fellowship.

I enjoyed my Sunday School class at the little church, Elim Chapel. Although only one of the families had a girl near my age, a church bus picked up a number of children, so there was a group of us the same age. The others were whisked away by the bus right after Sunday School while the church families stayed for a church service. One little girl, a toddler named Vurnell Newgard, would cross paths with me several times later in our lives. In one sense I felt comfortable with the people of Elim Chapel, as they seemed to be acceptable to my parents. Although some of the women had short hair like Lois, they compensated by wearing hats to church. I felt that these people were of the same "in-group" as my family. However soon a serious difficulty arose.

The Sunday School opening exercises were led by one of the Bible School students who urged pupil participation in the form of volunteering Bible verses, testimonies of God's working in our lives, and leading out in prayer. We children for the most part were very hesitant to volunteer, and so we were told that the devil was sitting on our laps, keeping us from standing up and speaking out for the Lord. I didn't mind standing up and saying Bible verses, but it scared the daylights out of me to even think of standing up with a testimony or leading out in prayer. We were taught that memorized prayers were not approved. My prayers at home were a statement of thanks for our blessings, or the recital of a list of relatives to be blessed. Somehow those prayers did not seem appropriate for Sunday School. I knew the stories of my parent's salvation experiences, but that had happened years before I was born and had nothing to do with me personally. My parents frequently got up in the church testimony meetings and told those stories in great length and detail. Nothing else was happening in our lives, except that we had food, clothes, and a house to live in. I didn't have anything to say in public to God or about Him.

To make things worse, when response was slow, the leader would turn to me and say with a sweet smile, "I'm sure Patty has a testimony for the Lord," or "I'm sure Patty will lead us in prayer." I was the oldest child of the six participating families, except for the pastor's teenaged boys who sat in the back glowering and obviously uncooperative. Since I was a quiet, sweet-looking child, bright in the Sunday School class and adept at repeating Bible verses, the leader thought I must have a vital relationship with God. When pressed like this, I had to say something, but it was fabricated, did not ring true even to me, and I became terribly upset. Soon I was waking up on Sunday morning with nausea or a severe headache. Sometimes I could talk my parents into letting me stay home, but more often I was made to go to church anyway. Soon just entering the little chapel made me feel sick to my stomach.

The Sunday evening services were also difficult for me. The pastor and his wife were converted Catholics, who were converted by hearing a sermon on the terrors of the end times from the book of Revelation. A favorite theme was the Great Tribulation coupled with much emphasis on "hell, fire, and brimstone." Another favorite theme was the "rapture of the church." My parents loved this kind of preaching. They sat there with their solid conversion experiences years behind them, their strong belief in "eternal security," a doctrine that says that once you have been saved, you can never be lost. It seemed to me that they and all the other adults reveled in hearing all the awful details of hell and the tribulation of which they were sure they would have no part. To their credit I could see that this was what drove my dad to pour himself tirelessly into his Gospel Car ministry and drove my mother to try to get everyone she met to pray the sinner's prayer.

However for me, the teaching on the rapture was the last straw. It was supposed to be our "blessed hope," but it was incredibly terrifying for me to think of my mother and father being taken to heaven "in the twinkling of an eye," leaving me all alone to go through the horrors of the Great Tribulation. I had no doubt that sweet little Dorothe and baby Darrell would also go, but it never even occurred to me that I might go too. I decided that my best hope was to never be too far from my mother, and if she started to go up, grab her quickly and hang on for dear life.

This fear became an obsession with me and was never far from my mind. It was not only the little chapel that fed my fear. About this time, Mother opened her home to Child Evangelism classes where all the same problems were repeated and intensified. Horror of horrors, when our class was asked to furnish a child to pray in front of the entire combined Twin City classes on Rally Day in the big First Baptist Church, I was chosen. My mother was pleased, and I dared not refuse. I still remember the red ribbons in my hair, and the terrible nausea in my stomach. Part of my problem was the natural phenomena of stage fright, but even worse was the feeling of being an absolute hypocrite, feeling that my words did not pass the ceiling, and that I really was not on speaking terms with God. We were also taken during those years to a number of camp meetings and other special conference-type services. World War II was starting. Hitler and Mussolini were more than plausible candidates for the Anti-Christ. The reoccurring topic in the sermons was usually the one that scared me so tremendously — the rapture and the great tribulation.

One night during the year that I was eight, when this terror was just starting, I went to my parents' bedroom, awakened them, and tried to tell them how I felt. At first Mother tried to tell me that I was fine, that I had not yet reached the "age of accountability," which she thought was probably about 12. When I wouldn't accept that approach, one of my parents explained to me that God and Satan both wanted to have me and that it was up to me to choose. We all got down on our knees beside the bed with me in the middle, and I told God I wanted to choose Him.

I wish I could tell you that that was the end of the matter. It was just the beginning. I slept that night, and I may have had some measure of peace for a few days, but soon the terror overwhelmed me again. Broaching the subject again with my mother only drew a strong admonition to not doubt my salvation. She assigned me to read the book of I John in the Bible and underline the word *know*. The word certainly occurred many times. I knew that my mother was firm in her knowledge of personal salvation, but nothing spoke to my heart. Now I had a bigger problem than before. I felt I could never mention my fears to anyone again.

During the day, a dark cloud of gloom hung over my head, but alone at night, the terror got really bad. Lying in bed awake was horrible, but sleep brought nightmares. The only way I could sleep peacefully was cuddled up beside my mother, hanging onto her as tightly as I could. It must have been difficult for Mother to have her oldest child behaving this way, and I imagine she never did really understand what was the matter with me.

Soon I started to have a negative reaction to anything Biblical or religious. I still enjoyed the Old Testament stories of Abraham, Moses, and David, but anything about Jesus brought the nausea and terror. The writings of the Apostle Paul could be tolerated, but anything written by Saint John upset me. In sixth grade we studied medieval artists, and the religious paintings of that era were too much for me. One famous painting of the crucifixion caused me about a month of anguished nights. I couldn't even bear to take a peek at the print we were required to purchase and paste in a notebook. I had to keep it covered with a piece of heavy paper.

At various times I tried to face the problem and solve it. I developed an aversion to my dad's Gospel Car, but one day I sat in my dad's brown leather chair that dominated the back of the van and read every tract on salvation that he had in his tract rack. There must have been ten or more. I tried to do everything that was suggested. I followed all the steps, prayed all the prayers, and tried to have the right feelings (although I was told over and over again in the tracts that feelings didn't matter; they ignored the "feeling" mentioned in Romans 8:16 *The Spirit itself beareth witness with our spirit, that we are the children of God)*. No matter what I did, it really didn't seem to make much difference. I would have a measure of peace for a few days, and then a sermon or something would trigger the terror again. Just when I thought I was making some progress I would overhear Mother and Dad discussing some acquaintance and commenting that they didn't think that person was "really saved," then I would think that if that person was deceived, I certainly was too, and I would be down in the depths again. Once I got up in the middle of the night, wrote my name and the date on a piece of paper, and filed it in my top dresser drawer with my few treasures. This was an attempt to "drive a stake" as I had read in one tract. (The idea was to drive a stake in your backyard and write the date

Dorothe, Darrell, & Patty about 1939.

that you prayed the sinners' prayer. When doubt came, you just went out and looked at the stake.) But it didn't help.

Finally I hit on an idea! Of course, I couldn't feel saved. I had never committed a bad enough sin to really feel like a sinner. The first step in all the salvation tracts was: I am a sinner. Of course! That must be my problem! I must do something really bad!

My parents made us wear long cotton stockings to school long after that custom had gone out of style.
Here I am in my gym uniform.

Chapter 5

A Futile Repentance

We had passed through the depression years without feeling the pinch of poverty, but now in about 1940, mother was starting to find it more difficult to make ends meet. Although Dad's job with the Post Office eventually led to promotions, culminating in a position as superintendent of the building, it had been a step down for Dad, both in pay and in personal satisfaction. Dad keenly felt the lack of a college or even a high school education. At Westinghouse he had been holding a job much beyond that which his educational achievement should have warranted. He often bragged to us, his family, that his practical mechanical skill had given him an advantage even over graduate engineers. He had no fear of heights or tight little places and could do repair and construction duties that others feared to tackle. Life with Westinghouse had been an adventure — new cities, new rescue missions, new friends, and challenging work. Now he was stuck with the routine maintenance of elevators at the Post Office. He became more cross and irritable in the brief times he was home with us. I had picked up enough of adult conversations to feel that I was the cause of his unhappiness. He had given up the job he loved so that I could have a stable life.

Mother still received half of the paycheck, but with three growing children to support and Grandma and other relatives taking refuge in our home from time to time, she was forced to administer the funds wisely without too many frills. While family meals were ample and nutritious, Mother did not believe in a lot of sweets. At dad's insistence we observed the Swedish custom of coffee or milk and a doughnut or other baked snack midmorning and midafternoon when he was home, but other than that, Mother carefully controlled our diet. Once in awhile, as a special treat, she gave us a penny to spend.

Oh, the joy of running as fast as our legs would go, straight to the Penny Shop two blocks away. The proprietor of this store was tall, thin, gray-haired Mr. Jepson. Standing in front of the large glass display case with its two shelves of goodies, any one of which could be bought by the copper coin clutched in our sweaty fists, kindly Mr. Jepson waited patiently while we carefully made our selection. Then we slowly sauntered home again, slowly sucking our goody, being careful to avoid the cracks and holes in the sidewalk in keeping with our childhood superstition, "step on a crack, break your mother's back, step in a hole, break your mother's sugar bowl," which we learned from the neighbor children.

On the other side of Mr. Jepson's store, across from the display of penny candy, was a small soda fountain. On Sunday afternoons when Dad was home, I would suggest to Dorothe that she ask Dad if we could have a treat. (It occurs to me now that he must have spent every other Sunday with us after the Saturday when he went to the Post Office. Then the next weekend he would be out with the Gospel Car.) I was so irritated with Dad that I hated to ask him for money. Most likely he would dig into his ample pocket and come out with two nickels, one for each of us. This time the purchase would be made on the soda fountain side of the store — two double-dip ice cream cones.

If by some strange good fortune, I could get hold of a nickel on a week day, I would immediately run to the Variety shop, across the street from Mr. Jepson's store, and buy five cent's worth of chocolate candy. The delicious treat was scooped out of a bin and weighed on a small scale — just the right amount for a nickel. Chocolate candy was my greatest weakness. My first recorded prayer in my satin-covered baby book was: Dear Lord, Bless Aunt Gladys 'cause she makes chocolate candy for Patty.

On the day that I decided I needed to commit a really bad sin, I sneaked into Mother's bedroom during lunch hour, and opened her purse. Passing up the pennies, nickels, and dimes, I clutched a quarter. More money than I had ever had before. Making a guilty retreat from the room, I grabbed my sweater, and ran down to the variety shop where I traded my quarter for a bag of chocolate five times as large as I had ever had before. It looked like a mountain heaped on the little scale. I don't remember having any trouble consuming the candy before the afternoon session of school opened, and I didn't even get a stomachache. That night with great anticipation I knelt at my bed to repent and be converted. To my great disappointment, it did not achieve the effect that I had desired. I didn't find the peace I sought. Mother never missed the quarter, but years later, when it really didn't matter anymore, I confessed the incident to her.

Eventually a disagreement between Dad and the pastor's wife caused us to quit attending the little church. I can't say that I was sorry. After a few years of home meetings, which I shamefully admit I sabotaged as often as possible (by being so slow to get myself into the living room that my parents got out of the mood and went off to do something else), Mother started taking us to a different church. She had listened to the pastor on the radio and liked his teachings. This was a large, well-organized church quite a bit farther away from our house. The doctrine held by the pastor (judged from the radio ministry) was close enough to Dad's that he would permit our attendance, but not close enough that he, himself, would attend. On the Sundays he spent in Minneapolis, he started taking his Gospel Car down to the corner of 7th and Hennepin, one of the main intersections of downtown Minneapolis. While leaving the truck in a prominent parking

54   Minnesota Mom in the Land of the Ancient Mother
Part Two: A Vision is Formed

spot to "do the preaching," he and his cronies would gather in a nearby cafeteria to drink coffee and "fellowship."

This started a custom that Dad continued until he was too old to drive anymore in 1980. His Gospel Car and tract rack became a fixture of the Minneapolis inner-city scene. Seekers or inquirers could easily be directed to the cafeteria to talk with Dad, and a core of like-minded men rallied around him.

Meanwhile, I was more or less unnoticed in the large Sunday School. I soon found the well-stocked church library where I started working on my goal of reading all the books.

I didn't enjoy the thin, Swedish pancakes that my mother
made for the rest of the family, but I just loved the ones
made from the Aunt Jemima ready-mix. From about
8 years old I made my own. I tried to eat as many as
Little Black Sambo, but I could never hold more than nine.

Chapter 6

Clouds of Turmoil

In school, problems were developing for me, not scholastically, but socially. I had been happy and well adjusted in the early years. We studied the native people of North America in second grade, and I had written a drama about the life of an Indian family. The teacher was so impressed that she assigned me a cast of my classmates to enact the script and sent us to an empty classroom to practice. The resulting play was presented not only to our class, but also to the entire school in assembly. Later we even repeated it for the parents. This was such a successful experience that it was decided to continue the effort, and this same small group of children presented a drama each semester. I never authored another play, but I remember starring as Alice in Wonderland. However by the time I was in sixth grade, the overwhelming torment that was raging in my heart evidenced itself on my face. I was beginning to revert to reading to escape and temporarily lift the dark cloud. I lived in my own world, largely unaware of the social intricacies of my classmates.

One time the most popular girl in our class took an interest in me as her special friend. She walked towards home with me day after day, talking of the wonderful party she was giving for her birthday, taking me into her plans on a most intimate level. However on the day of the much-anticipated party, I was curled up on the sofa in my oldest clothes, deeply engrossed in my book, when the telephone rang. It was my friend, wondering why I hadn't shown up at her party. I had forgotten about it. Mother drove me to her house as soon as I could get ready, but the party was almost over by the time I arrived. My self-inflicted solitude had sabotaged my opportunity, and the budding relationship with this girl was never restored.

I guess I was also getting into an awkward age. My long curly hair that had caused so many compliments was now getting frizzy and unmanageable, especially since Mother would not allow even the split ends to be trimmed away. I had a peculiar walk as a result of a mild congenital hip problem, and this was no longer cute. Because of my hip condition, I was not especially good in athletics, although I excelled in running and the high jump. In fact I am afraid I appeared quite clumsy.

My family's dress code, while not so hard on a small child, was now starting to isolate me and make me appear different from my schoolmates. To further complicate the situation, in spite of years of piano and violin lessons, I couldn't carry a tune. In the Minneapolis schools, which were very music-oriented, I had to sit up in front with the monotones and out-of-tune singers in music class.

People were starting to say in my hearing, "Dorothe is the pretty one of the family, isn't she?" The irrational fears of my early childhood escalated to the status of phobias. I found escape from my unhappy present by identifying more and more deeply with the lives of the fictional characters in my books. I read my favorite stories over and over and fantasized, writing sequels in my mind to the books I most loved. I loved history and tried to put myself back in former days by writing historical novels in my mind. Of course when Dad was home, I had to be seen only reading the Bible or *Hurlbert's Story of the Bible*. Many times I locked myself in the bathroom for hours with my book, or hid out of sight under the bed or behind the sofa to immerse myself in a make-believe world.

Mother was one of those ageless persons. Her hair had always been gray, ever since I could first remember. She always wore glasses for her nearsightedness. She never paid any attention to style but always looked "neat and nice." Even in her eighties, she still had her own teeth and had changed very little from my early memories. On the other hand Dad, once boyishly handsome with his blue eyes and curly blond hair, came into a midlife crisis. His hair thinned out; he needed glasses; his teeth were replaced by dentures. At each stage we were regaled at the dinner table with a detailed account of the miseries of growing older. We were sternly admonished to take good care of our eyes, teeth, and hair. Finally my long list of aversions extended to him too. I couldn't stand his crabby, negative attitude. On top of my already morose anxieties, he was too much to bear. I began to avoid him as much as possible. The loss to me was great and to him as well, but neither one of us knew how to make the situation improve. I know I would often sit and glare at him (I never dared or knew how to voice my feelings), and he would call me the "offended princess," not having a clue as to why I was offended. For many years we lived parallel lives in the same house, seldom making contact in any meaningful manner.

Outwardly I was submissive and obedient, but the inward stress was tearing me apart. Finally the emotional and spiritual strain manifested itself in a physical way. In the summer of 1941, I broke out in severe hives every morning at nine o'clock. Avoidance of strawberries and tomatoes did no good, nor did any other remedy. My life had just become too difficult. The itchy red blotches surrounded by rough purple skin started to fade about noon each day. Overtly, I was worried about the move to junior high school the following January. I knew that great changes would be required in my life. Would

I be able to meet them? Inwardly, the spiritual struggle continued; it was always just below the surface.

Lois faded out of our lives just when I needed her most. We waved her off on the train to California, little realizing that she had gone out of our lives practically forever. We would not see her again until we had children of our own. A few years later, Grandma Winburn fell, broke her hip, and died of pneumonia. I would go into junior high school and adolescence in emotional isolation — close to no one except Mother, whose country background gave her little understanding of the trials her inexperienced and emotionally upset daughter was about to undergo in a big city junior high school. It was enough to make anyone break out in hives.

Pat, Dorothe, & Darrell - 1941 About this time
I dropped the "Patty" in favor of "Pat" as a nickname.

Chapter 7

The Darkness Before Dawn

Junior high school memories are etched in my mind in shades of black and gray. Six weeks before we started seventh grade, the bombing of Pearl Harbor had plunged the United States into World War II. My terror of hell had come closer to home. On a large map in my geography classroom island after island in the South Pacific was colored yellow as they fell to the Japanese, and I shuddered with fear. Daylight savings time was imposed in January to save energy, and we left home for the mile-long walk to the junior high school in the frigid darkness of the Minnesota winter morning well before the sun made its appearance.

Because of my extra promotion in first grade, I was young for my school grade and socially under-developed besides. My only confidant was a girl from my grade school that I will call Molly. She had registered as a new student in our sixth grade at midyear, and I had befriended her. Now she walked to school with me each morning. She bolstered her ego by telling me all the negative comments, which she said our classmates were making about me. It never occurred to me to mistrust her motives.

According to Molly, I was despised for my lack of make-up, my meager, outmoded wardrobe, and my hairstyle of long corkscrew curls. Also, I was ignorant concerning movie stars and popular music since I wasn't allowed to attend movies or listen to the radio. These daily walks with Molly convinced me that I was disliked by my peers, and fearing overt rejection, I buried myself even more deeply in books from the school library, rarely speaking to anyone. I managed to preserve a bit of self-esteem by excelling scholastically.

Dorothe and me just before our piano recital.
We were not very talented musically, but Mother did all she could for us.

Fears that the rapture would occur and take my parents while I was at school still tormented me, but my mind finally figured out a solution. Deducing that surely God would not leave tiny children without their parents but would take them along, a glance out the window that revealed preschoolers playing in their yards would put my mind at rest, convinced that the fearsome day had not yet arrived.

However, now a new terror started tormenting me. A weekly program was presented in the school auditorium. Many times these presentations consisted of moving pictures, sometimes classics, but usually a western and a newsreel. I had never been allowed to see movies, and television had not yet appeared, so to me the sight of people being shot and killed right in front of my eyes in the western films was exceedingly horrifying. But worse were the newsreels showing battle scenes and executions by firing squad. The sight of these made me ill for days. Night after night I tossed sleeplessly with the movies replaying in my mind. At the end of ninth grade my parents wisely decided to enroll me in Minnehaha Academy, a private Christian high school run by the Swedish Mission Covenant denomination.

In our last semester of junior high, we had been required to choose our life occupation so that our last years of high school could be wisely planned. I had agonized over this decision and was the last in the class to settle on a choice. I was secretly interested in becoming a teacher but did not dare to brave the ridicule of my peers by naming such an unpopular profession. Finally, in desperation I had settled on being a dietitian but was happy to scrap that plan now. The Academy did not give much choice of subjects, concentrating on a college preparatory program.

As in many small Christian schools, cliquishness was a major problem at the Academy. The cliques had been established at the beginning of ninth grade, and latecomers found it difficult to enter the existing ranks. I didn't even try to break in but was happy to eat lunch with three or four other girls who had also started at midterm. Even this was social progress for me since in junior high I had buried myself in a book and munched my sandwiches alone.

The chapel services at the Academy had a different atmosphere than our church. I was impressed by the large number of young people, older than myself, who would stand up voluntarily to lead singing, testify or pray. Testimony opportunities met with great response. Twenty or thirty boys and girls would jump to their feet at the first opportunity and stand quietly awaiting their turns. Many of my classmates came to school a half hour before classes to join in a voluntary time of prayer on their knees in a vacant classroom. There had been an outpouring of the Spirit of God, a revival, the year before

62 Minnesota Mom in the Land of the Ancient Mother
Part Two: A Vision is Formed

The three of us in 1942. Dad would have liked to have us sing from the back of his Gospel car, but it just didn't work.

I started the Academy, and the effects were still being felt. Soon after I entered the school, a visiting chapel speaker requested that all who wanted to indicate that their lives were completely dedicated to God come to the front. Over half the student body responded, and I was among them. I went home happy that afternoon. The first light was starting to break through the dark clouds.

Several months before my transfer to Minnehaha Academy, "Youth for Christ" started holding Saturday night rallies in the huge Minneapolis Auditorium. Since Dad approved of large, citywide interdenominational functions, and Mother sensed our need for Christian contacts, our parents were very faithful in taking us to these rallies. Looking out over the audience at the many gray and white heads, we sometimes laughed at the name and suggested that "Old Folks for Christ" might be a more appropriate name. However, judging from the huge crowds and the enthusiasm generated by these rallies, it is certain that they filled a need for the Minneapolis evangelical community. Here we were offered a mixture of entertainment and challenge, but most of all, we saw a visual representation of the Invisible Church of Greater Minneapolis.

Looking out over the vast crowd that gathered Saturday after Saturday in the huge auditorium, I knew that my junior high school teachers and classmates were not right. Evangelical Christianity was not something outdated, but pulsating and vibrant. My heart thrilled as we all rose to our feet to sing:

He lives! He lives! Christ Jesus lives today!
He walks with me, and talks with me,
Along life's narrow way.
He lives! He lives! Salvation to impart.
You ask me how I know He lives,
He lives within my heart!

I knew that He lived in my mother's heart, and how I longed to know that He lived in mine too. Only fear of my parents' disapproval kept me from going down the aisle when the invitation was given.

Eva, Dick, Auntie Mal, Uncle Eddy
Dorothe, Pat, Darrell and Daniel.
The two families on vacation.

64   Minnesota Mom in the Land of the Ancient Mother
      Part Two: A Vision is Formed

Pat about 1943.

Chapter 8

First Rays of Light

Spring changed into summer. It was a beautiful day in July 1945. World War II had ended on the European front. Rays of morning sunlight danced on the sparkling waters of Lake Nokomis. Mother Eva spread a blanket under a big tree where she and a neighbor lady would sit and chat while we girls had a swim. This was our first trip to the beach this year since we had all been down with the mumps. Dorothe and I had both been very ill with complications.

Over the sand and into the water we raced. While Dorothe hung back in the shallow water, twelve-year-old Mary, a neighbor girl, and I struck out for the diving raft some 25 yards from the shore. In the car on the way to the beach, we had discussed the possibility of Mary reaching the raft safely. Although the same age as Dorothe, Mary was large and strong. She decided to make the attempt since I assured her that I could help her should she get too tired. She had never swum to the raft before, but I had been doing it for several years.

Suddenly, about two-thirds of the way to the raft, a horrible weakness clutched my entire body. I knew I would never make it. My heavy limbs frantically went into an involuntary dog paddle, rapidly using up the slight energy I had left. I knew this was the end. My mother was far away on the shore, completely unaware that I was in danger. Frightened, Mary tried to help me, but I told her that it was no use and calmly bade her goodbye. My arms and legs would not quit paddling, but I was inhaling water now, and my head was more under water than above. At the last minute, I felt the grip of a strong arm. A young man on the raft had seen my plight, plunged in, and pulled me over to the ladder. Lying face down on the raft, gasping for breath as the water drained out of my mouth and nose, I struggled with a new thought. I had been face-to-face with death and had not been frightened. In Calvinistic terms I guess I could say, I felt that a little of the grace of God was working in my life. Anyway, for the first time I had some hope.

When school started again in the fall, I decided to put the gloomy thoughts aside. I must be as much "saved" as anyone else, I thought. I started attending the morning prayer meetings and even led out with a prayer from my heart occasionally. I really enjoyed the chapel services, learning to sing some of the fine old hymns of the more formal arm of the church and standing to testify occasionally, even if I had to lift phrases out of other testimonies and put them together.

We children and Mother continued to attend Bethesda church regularly. While only a medium-sized congregation, the Sunday School was large with over nine hundred on the roll. The adult class was taught by the pastor, H. B. Prince. Chugging west after church in our 1939 Plymouth, Mother tried to share with us children the glorious teachings she was receiving. Much was said about a mystery that was revealed to the Apostle Paul and was only understood by those of us holding to the ultra-dispensational theology. It assured us of a top place in heaven according to Mother. In contrast, my Sunday School class seemed to only repeat the things I had learned in my early childhood from my parents and at Elim Chapel. I loved my Sunday School teachers and made one good friend among the girls, Marlys.

If my Sunday School was humdrum, the same could not be said of the Bethesda Sunday Morning Service. Soon I was allowed to sit in the balcony with Marlys. Mrs. Rheinholt skillfully handled the organ; the robed choir filed into their places. Last of all came Pastor Prince, followed by the music director. Humor and seriousness were skillfully mingled in the services. The atmosphere was entertaining, but never frivolous nor boisterous. Looking back through the corridor of the years since I left Bethesda, I marvel at the fine line of balance that was maintained. I have never since seen it duplicated.

H. B. Prince, a velvet-throated orator with a well-developed talent of tasteful showmanship, dominated the scene. Distinctive of features and impeccably dressed, his rotund figure emitted an aura of mystery. Even the giving of the announcements, a task despised by most preachers, was used as a platform for Pastor Prince's oratorical skills. We were not clock-watchers. The announcements could take half an hour; the sermon was always at least forty-five minutes to an hour, or even longer. In a word Prince's preaching could be described as inspiring. While at the opposite pole doctrinally from anything that could be considered Pentecostal or charismatic, he was able to touch emotions in a deep and profound manner, raising his audience to heights of commitment or ecstasy as he interpreted Romans, Ephesians, and other Pauline writings.

We young people knew nothing of the pastor's private life, not even where he lived. Mrs. Prince, a refined looking woman of Danish extraction, sat properly in one of the front pews each Sunday but played no active part in the affairs of the church. The Princes had no children.

My father, however, was not impressed. "The man is a talking machine," commented Dick after a Sunday service that Mother talked him into attending. He preferred to take his Gospel Car downtown on Sunday mornings. "The car does the preaching," he told us, "while I fellowship with my friends."

Pastor Prince was extremely missions-minded. We were often treated to a presentation of missionary slides or movies on Sunday evenings. A large world map in the sanctuary displayed the church's missions outreach, and a large placard announced the church's policy of giving half of every dollar to missions. Most of the mission work was among primitive tribes in South America. However the pastor was very impressed with a young couple that had gone to Ethiopia as teachers with the intention of informally carrying on a Christian witness as well. Pastor Prince called them "Tentmakers". They were going out in the tradition of the Apostle Paul as self-supporting missionaries.

The summer of 1946 three friends from Minnehaha Academy and I spent a week at the second annual Youth for Christ Conference, which was held at the Medicine Lake Campground just outside Minneapolis. The campgrounds were familiar to me, as my parents had often taken us there to hear special speakers, but this was my first time there as a camper. The fledgling Youth for Christ movement was just getting underway, and the week was packed full with messages from young preachers who were later to become big names in the Christian world. Billy Graham, Cliff Barrows, George Wilson, and George Beverly Shea, all to achieve fame later in the Billy Graham Crusades, were just starting their ministries with a send-off for England. Bob Pierce, later to found World Vision, was planning to lead a team to the Far East. Dawson Trotman brought teaching on Bible memorization and study. He would later develop the Navigator System of memory work.

Although clouded a bit by doctrinal disputes with my roommates in the large Indian Wigwam that served as a girls' dormitory, this week was a watershed experience in my early life. I felt that I had to defend my dad's beliefs against my friends' Lutheran and Covenant orientation. I surprised everyone and myself as well by having a long, hysterical crying spell one afternoon after trying to defend the doctrine of eternal security. This attack astounded me, as I had not cried since I was in first grade. (Up until that time I had been known as a "crybaby." I remember standing on the school playground and making a vow to myself that I would never cry again.)

The theology that I had always been taught and was trying to defend went as follows: First, one had to realize that he was a sinner. Secondly, he had to believe that Jesus died to save sinners. Thirdly, the gift of salvation had to be received by faith. This experience, referred to as "being born again," "being saved," or "being converted" insured that you were a child of God and could never again be "lost." My colossal struggle had been to know whether or not I had actually had this experience so that I could "claim" all the wonderful benefits as described so eloquently Sunday after Sunday by Pastor Prince. Now my three friends, who had been exposed to a slightly different theology, were bringing up questions I had never yet considered, such as: What about a man who having been "saved" as a child, commits murder and dies before he can repent? Finally in frustration and confusion I sobbed hysterically while they looked on astounded.

I pulled myself together for supper and the evening service. That night we were treated to a preview of the now familiar Billy Graham meeting. After a rousing songfest led by the young, handsome Cliff Barrows, an offering taken by George Wilson, and a stirring bass solo by tall, rugged-looking George Beverly Shea, a young blond Billy came to the pulpit. At the end of his message came his now famous altar call. As the congregation softly sang "Just As I am" men, women, and young people streamed forward. Altar calls were frequently given at Bethesda church and at the Minneapolis

Part Two: A Vision is Formed

Youth for Christ, but only a scattered few responded. I had never seen anything like this before. I longed to join them to see if something the handsome young preacher would say to the seekers would give me the mystical assurance that I so desperately sought, but after the events of the afternoon, I did not want to indicate to my friends that I was unsure of my own salvation. Suddenly, as the meeting was being dismissed, I had an idea. Billy was taking the seekers up on the platform to the seats vacated by the choir. The tabernacle wall behind the chairs was made of screening.

"Come with me a minute," I whispered to Marian, one of my friends. Together we ran around to the back of the tabernacle where we could hear through the screen without being seen. My friend could see no point in this and wanted to leave, but I stayed long enough to satisfy myself that nothing was being said that I didn't already know.

The next evening Bob Pierce spoke on missions. His heart was breaking for the suffering of the Far East in the aftermath of World War II. His text was taken from Matthew 24:14: *And this gospel of the kingdom shall be preached in all the world for a witness unto all nations; and then shall the end come.* At the close of his message, he gave an impassioned plea for people to come forward to dedicate themselves to the foreign field. He clearly stated that he was not just asking for an indication of willingness to go, should God call them but was addressing those who could say: "I know that God is calling me to go to the foreign field, and I intend to go." I felt a strong tug at my heart and stepped out into the aisle. Marian was already there, and together we passed to the front where we were prayed for by Bob Pierce.

After the service, as we joined our friends for a bottle of soda pop, I felt a joy in my heart and a peace that I had never before known. It was as though God were smiling at me. "Of course," I thought. "That's why I couldn't settle on a career choice in ninth grade. I'm supposed to be a missionary." The last few days of camp were a spiritual feast for me. On Sunday I went home with a box of memory verse cards and a notebook of profound and pithy quotes from the conference speakers. One example — an answer to critics who would tell us we were wasting our lives and missing a lot of fleshly fun for an uncertain goal of spiritual reward – "I would rather chase a rabbit and fail, than chase a skunk and catch it."

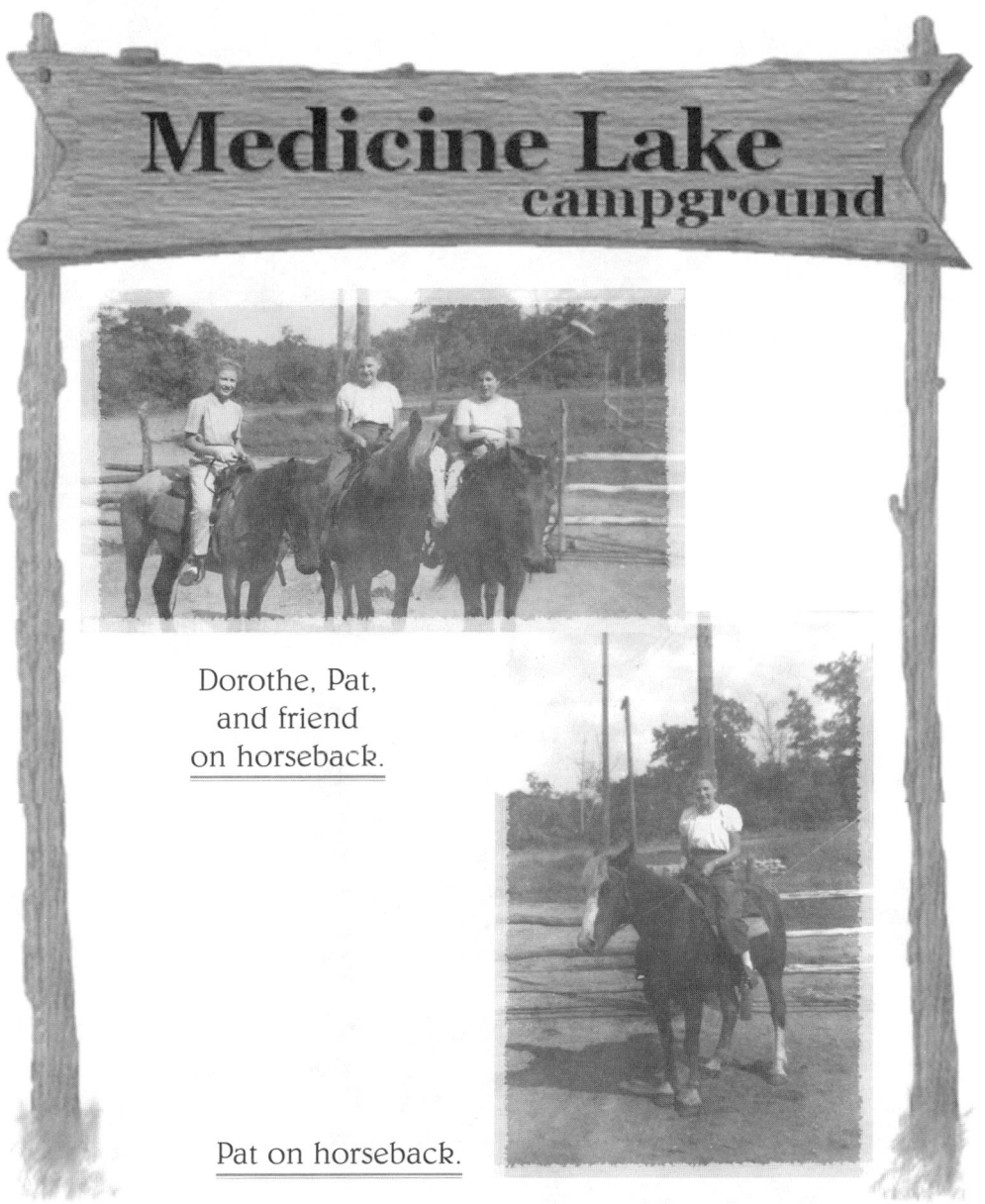

Dorothe, Pat, and friend on horseback.

Pat on horseback.

72   Minnesota Mom in the Land of the Ancient Mother
Part Two: A Vision is Formed

A friend and Pat.

Pat with my
high school friends.

We all attended
Minnehaha
Academy.

Chapter 9

The Vision Dashed

Back home, the Bible came alive to me. The verses on the memory cards selected from scattered Old Testament books were vibrant with meaning. *There is a way that seemeth right unto a man, but the ends thereof are the ways of death. They that wait upon the Lord shall renew their strength. . .*

I also started reading in the New Testament. Since I did not feel at ease reading in the Gospels, due to the ultra-dispensational teaching from my home and church, I started with Romans, the first book (per the New Testament order) written by the Apostle Paul. God started speaking to me in the first chapter, and I underlined in red the verses that were especially meaningful. My heart was warmed, and the Lord illuminated these verses to my heart. Soon I was memorizing these portions as well as the verses from my memory box. As Dawson Trotman had taught us, I reviewed regularly all the verses previously studied and spent time meditating on each verse. Since all this was done at night after everyone else had gone to bed, the only place I dared turn on the light was in the bathroom.

At first my parents didn't notice, but as my list grew, they started to wonder why I was spending so much time in the bathroom. For some reason I didn't want them to know what I was doing, so when they insisted that I go to bed, I tried continuing my study by flashlight with my head under the covers. Eventually I was discovered, and thinking that I was ruining my eyes by reading novels after bedtime, they strictly monitored my bedtime activities and saw to it that I went to sleep by nine.

Soon after I returned from Medicine Lake, Dad took me aside and told me that he had been present at the camp the evening that Bob Pierce preached and had noticed that I had responded to the altar call. While indicating a certain approval of my expressed desire to obey God, he gently revealed to me that present day missions were not acceptable to his theology. He especially disliked Pierce's emphasis that the second coming of Christ was dependent upon the preaching of the gospel to the world. To my sixteen-year-old mind, God and my father were so united that it never occurred to me that Dad could be in error. I decided that Bob Pierce must have made a mistake and humbly suggested that Dad teach me all that he knew. From that time on, I became my father's disciple, sitting at his feet so to speak, as he explained to me his ultra-dispensational interpretation of the Bible. To Dad at that time, missions was a sinister plan of the devil to ship as many as possible of the best Christians out of the United States and England to the barren wastelands where they could do little harm.

I accepted all that Dad taught me unquestioningly, and when I returned to school in the fall for my senior year (I had leaped ahead another half year at the Academy, so that I could graduate in June—they had no January graduation), I tried to promote his viewpoint in my Bible classes. I was quite shy and did not really cause a problem, but as I recounted the incidents across the dinner table, Dad beamed with pride, and I felt that I had started to exist as a person worthy of esteem in his eyes.

Although my vision for missions was put on the back burner for a while, some major changes took place in my life at this point: I started to come out of the dream world of fantasy I had built for myself. I spent less time reading fiction, and

The Vision Dashed   75

started reading some of the books of theology that my dad recommended. My relationship with my dad took a turn for the better. We now had some times of meaningful conversation around the dinner table. I began to smile more. I learned from one of the advice-to-teenagers columns in our daily newspaper the importance of a smile. I realized that I was very deficient in that area; in fact I tended to glare at people, sure that they were going to reject me and prefer someone else. I began to make a conscious effort to smile at people, especially my classmates at school. It did make a difference. I began to spend more time in light conversation and less time with my nose buried in a book. Soon I was actually feeling more like smiling.

We continued to attend the Youth for Christ rallies on Saturday evenings. A gospel team was being readied to minister in China just before communism closed the door. An urgent plea was made for sacrificial offerings to fund the venture. My parents had opened a savings account at a local bank for each of us children at our birth and had made small deposits from time to time. I now possessed around two hundred dollars in this account. (Of course this was worth more in 1946 than it would be today.) Every time the appeal was made for donations for China, I felt a tug at my heart to withdraw all or part of my money from the bank and donate it to this cause. However I never mustered up enough courage to present the proposal to my parents, knowing that Mother's frugality and Dad's aversion to foreign missions would lead them to disapprove of the idea.

To salve my conscience, I decided to deny myself the occasional ice cream cone or other nickel treat that came my way and put the money in the offering for China. In this manner, I was able to accumulate the magnificent sum of seventy-five cents. Somehow my endeavor became known within the family, and Dad's pride knew no bounds. He was extremely impressed that his daughter was actually practicing self-denial, but I felt guilty and disobedient before God.

My high school graduation picture - 1947.

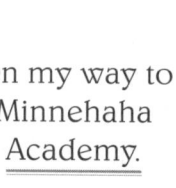

On my way to Minnehaha Academy.

Chapter 10

College

"Girl! You are going to go to school until you are an old woman!" My father periodically reiterated this, usually through clenched teeth. Dad's intense emotion left me no alternative but to plan on college. During his years installing elevators in skyscrapers, Dad had resented taking orders from young whippersnappers in black engineers' boots with half his age and experience. He was galled to the core that their college degrees opened doors that his innate mechanical genius could not. Young as I was, I realized that he was trying to fulfill his frustrated ambitions through me, but as I loved to study and wanted to go to college, no problem existed. He had stamped on my mind at a young age that girls who did not get an education ended up in the kitchen of some restaurant washing unending stacks of dirty dishes. I was ready to go to college. The problem was which college, and what to study.

Ever since the unfortunate loss of their first child in Cincinnati, Dad had harbored an intense distrust of doctors, which had passed on to me in the form of a phobia of all that was medical. Dad strongly believed that the woman's place was in the home, and while he did grudgingly accept females as teachers, salespersons, and secretaries, he strongly disapproved of their entering male-dominated professions. Dad was not alone in this viewpoint, and while by the 1940's a number of women had entered the medical profession, they were battling for acceptance.

In view of this, I was extremely amazed when Dad announced that I was to go to medical school. Secretly, I was proud that Dad obviously made an exception for me from the rather low opinion he held of women in general, and I was too naive to realize the financial sacrifice on his part that would have been required to put me through medical school, but I instinctively felt that I was not prepared for the tremendous dedication to a career and investment of energy that would have been required to become a woman doctor in those days. I had not lost my dread of doctors, and although I was very reluctant to enter a career that involved the sight of blood and close proximity to doctors, I suggested nursing as a compromise, but this suggestion he refused without serious consideration. No daughter of his was going to spend her life carrying bedpans, he thundered. Finally, we more or less compromised on teaching as an acceptable career — neither one of us being really excited about it. I greatly feared the language requirement for most college degrees, including education. Four days of Spanish in junior high, and one year of Swedish at Minnehaha Academy had convinced me that my mouth was not designed to speak a foreign language.

I wanted to get away from home, feeling that I needed a change of environment, so I suggested Wheaton, a Christian college in Illinois. Dad, however, demanded that I attend a local school so that I could cut expenses by living at home (also, I was sure, he didn't want me to get out from under his thumb too quickly). His first choice was the University of Minnesota, but for my first year, I attended Augsburg, a Lutheran college where several of my friends from Minnehaha Academy were also registering.

This first year of college became a delightful time for me. For some reason, I suddenly 'clicked' socially. A beautician friend of my mother's had trimmed and shaped my unruly locks. I faithfully administered 100 strokes with a brush every night, and learned to use curlers, resulting in the pageboy style that was popular in the 1940's. I analyzed my figure problems and faithfully exercised by doing calisthenics down on the floor every night to get myself in shape. I tried to eat a lot of raw vegetables and cut down on the sweet pastries that I so loved. I had been working part-time at a bakery during my senior year and all summer and so had some savings set aside for my college wardrobe. Dad uncomplainingly paid all college fees and expenses that were presented to him, but my clothes had to come from my own earnings. Mother always provided sturdy school shoes and a warm winter coat out of her household allowance, but style and fashion were out of her line.

Truckin' the Good News

For 45 years **Dick and Eva Carlson** have been parking their gospel truck near 7th St. and Hennepin Av. in Minneapolis to lure uncertain souls back to the Lord.

Covered with Biblical quotes, the three trucks they've used over the years have quite literally been vehicles of their missionary zeal.

"We're just trying to reach people with the gospel," said Eva, 82. "We show them the good news."

Just after 6 p.m. six nights a week they drive downtown from their south Minneapolis home, find a parking spot on 7th St., have dinner in a nearby restaurant, then drive home. On Sundays they drive down in the morning, have breakfast, then take the bus home, leaving the truck on duty all day.

They have been following this routine almost daily for 15 years, since Dick, 83, retired as an elevator installer. Last year they missed just two days because of bad weather. Before parking became illegal on Hennepin they parked there to be in the midst of a street culture they've always felt has been "unhealthy."

Yet unlike the bold, three-inch lettering that shouts salvation from their camper, the Carlsons themselves are soft-spoken people. They describe themselves as nondenominational, "saved" Christians, and they won't push their beliefs on you. As Eva puts it, "What more can people do than present the gospel? It's up to the individual to accept or reject it."

They refuse to confront strangers on the street, nor will they ask for money or accept it if offered. "Doing that will sicken people of the gospel," Dick said.

Witnessing their faith has been the focal point of the Carlsons' 50-year marriage. Though neither was raised as a Christian, their conversions many years ago were such riveting experiences that they have always felt compelled to testify publicly.

After their marriage in 1928, Dick and Eva hopscotched around the country for five years. Dick installed elevators during the day, preached in missions at night and sometimes squeezed a little gospel in on the job, too. While Eva never preached, she was always eager to testify if asked.

The Carlsons liked the first Bible truck they saw, in Portland, Ore., shortly before moving to Minneapolis in 1933. Once here they ordered a white 1934

In 1979 this article about my parents
appeared in a Minneapolis magazine.

Part Two: A Vision is Formed

Dodge panel truck. After equipping it with six-foot trumpet horns, a turret loudspeaker atop the cab and gospel quotations painted on the sides, the Carlsons began their 45-year ministry.

The Carlsons are now on their third truck and have logged thousands of miles. For many years Dick also preached at the Union Gospel Mission in the St. James Hotel until the building was torn down. Eva still attends a weekly prayer meeting. Dick does not participate in any organized religious activity.

Their truck has caused varying reactions. "We have lots of friends who stop to see us," said Eva. "Not long ago a man stepped up who told us he first saw our truck 10 years ago. He was an alcoholic then, but he goes to church now. He told us our truck made him change his life."

They've also been heckled and sneered at, but most people who speak to them are friendly. "Lots of people come up and say thank you. That peps me up," said Eva.

—*Pat Kelly*

Eva and Dick Carlson and their gospel on wheels.

In 1979 this article about my parents appeared in a Minneapolis magazine.

The spiritual climate of the student body at Augsburg was considerably cooler than at the Academy, and my friends and I were soon considered among the more "spiritual." We were used to giving testimonies in chapel and leading out in public prayer, customs that were new to many of our classmates. This ability endeared us to many of the faculty and visiting pastors. Even though I tried to argue my ultra-dispensational viewpoint in the freshman Bible class, I did not seem to draw any animosity from the professors. Seemingly they admired and appreciated my interest in theology, even if I strayed from accepted Lutheran concepts. Some of our other classmates who were also spiritually oriented were the pre-seminary students. They studied Greek, and I became fascinated with the idea of taking Greek to fulfill my two-year foreign language requirement, especially after learning that *the speaking* of Greek was not required.

I joined the Missions Club, a group that presented programs in the rescue missions of the city. I felt good to be following in my father's footsteps, although I was quite handicapped for lack of a good singing voice. Still, I found I could make a contribution by reading a Scripture portion, leading in prayer, bringing a short testimony or devotional message or even accompanying the singing on the piano, if no one with more talent was available.

While maintaining B's and C's, my scholastic achievement was considerably lower than it was in high school. Instead of being serious, scholarly, and timid, I now presented a smiley, friendly image — slightly crazy and a little bit wild. I got a lot of attention that way. I'm sure my friends from the Academy were quite dismayed. Soon classmates were asking me for dates to social events. The first time I went out with a young man, I had to leave Mother weeping in a darkened bedroom, but she gradually became accustomed to the fact that her little daughter was going to have a social life.

Dorothe, Darrell & Pat about 1947.

I loved the atmosphere of the college campus. I made friends with girls from out of town who lived in the girls' dorm. Many times I spent the night with them in their rooms where we talked all night and took No-Doze tablets and drank black coffee to stay awake in class the next day. I pumped the girls who had more dating experience for guidelines on how far to go on a date. I found that most of them were more lenient and lax than I would have expected. However, the only time I found myself in a really compromising situation, verses from I Corinthians 6:18-20 that I had memorized in the bathroom after going to camp at Medicine Lake came back to me: *Flee fornication. Every sin that a man doeth is without the body; but he that commiteth fornication sinneth against his own body. What? Know ye not that your body is the temple of the Holy Ghost which is in you, which ye have of God, and ye are not your own? For ye are bought with a price: therefore glorify God in your body, and in your spirit, which is God's.* I quoted those verses to the young man, and asked him how he reconciled these verses with what he was proposing. He was a pastor's son, but he responded, "You leave the Bible out of this?" When I said I wouldn't, he took me directly home, and I was very careful whom I dated after that.

Imagine my chagrin when Christian Dior's "New Look" caught on half way through my first year of college. Hemlines dropped overnight from above the knee to mid-calf, making my entire wardrobe of carefully selected college skirts and suits obsolete. I was able to acquire two long skirts and three or four "Gibson girl" blouses, and with these finished the year. After the "New Look" came in, a girl wouldn't be caught dead in a short skirt.

At church, I still had a problem. Sunday School class assignments were strictly according to age, and one stayed in the high school group until his or her 18th birthday. Although I was not yet 18, I pleaded the fact that I was in college and started attending the Senior Young People's Society on Sunday Evenings. I escaped from the high school Sunday School class by volunteering to teach two-year-olds. One of my former Sunday School teachers went to Kentucky to work with the mountain children, and I was enthralled with the accounts of her work. I felt that this would most likely be my mission field, right in the United States, so how could my dad object.

After a few months at Augsburg, I became good friends with one of the second year pre-seminary students. We spent a lot of time together at the college, mostly accompanied by one of my friends from high school, Esther. He and Esther were both fun to be with, full of corny jokes, but yet with a deeply spiritual side. The young man was the son of foreign missionaries and had a little different outlook from the boys who had never been out of Minnesota. Of course the few times he came to my house, my father succeeded in embarrassing him. Dad, being so rigid in his views, could never pass up an opportunity to correct and humiliate someone who deviated from what to him was the obvious course of action. Whatever the reason, all of a sudden, with no explanation, this young man dropped out of my life completely. He avoided me as if I had the plague at school, and being a year ahead of me, we were in none of the same classes, so had no opportunity to meet causually. Although we were merely friends, this really hurt, but in those days a "nice" girl could make no advances — even a phone call was considered improper, so apart from dropping a note in his college post office box, which went unanswered, there was nothing I could do to mend our friendship.

(Fifty years later, a mutual friend encountered this man, now an elderly pastor. Somehow my name came up, and I believe our friend gave him one of our books. He revealed that he had known me but lost interest after I told him I wanted to be a missionary. In spite of having grown up on the mission field, he evidently did not have that calling.)

Although I never mentioned this hurt to anyone, Mother must have seen that I was grieving. One day driving to church, Mother said, "Why don't you go with that nice-looking blond boy in the choir?" In those days a girl didn't just "up and go" with someone, you had to be asked, so I responded, "Hmph, I wouldn't go out with him if he were the last one in the world."

Minnesota Mom in the Land of the Ancient Mother
Part Two: A Vision is Formed

Chad when I met him in 1947.

Chad was a very talented piano player.

Chapter 11

Chad Stendal

Even though it was my mother's suggestion, I did start taking note of the "nice looking blond boy." I found out that his name was Chad Stendal. He was new to Bethesda having recently been discharged from the U.S. Army. Although from an unchurched family, he had had a remarkable conversion experience just before being drafted. He had risen to the rank of Second Lieutenant and had spent almost a year in the South Pacific. Now he was a pre-engineering student at Macalester College in St. Paul, the sister city across the river from Minneapolis.

The Senior Young People's group met at 5:00 p.m. Sunday evenings. Following a lively meeting, a light supper was served in the church basement, allowing us all to be in the 7:30 evening service on time. At seventeen, I was the very youngest member of the group; the others were for the most part twenty and up; a number were veterans of World War II, who were taking advantage of the G. I. bill to continue their college education after military service. Our group had a basketball team that competed with other churches. I faithfully attended the games to root for our team, and especially for a tall, good-looking player, an ex-sailor, one of the older members of the group, whom I will call Bill. Unfortunately our team did not make it to the play-offs, but one Sunday evening in the winter of 1948, all the basketball team members were selling tickets to the final game. I had been sending out signals, hoping that the tall player would ask me to go to the game with him, but he did not seem to be aware of my existence.

As a number of us sat around in a circle on folding chairs eating our sandwiches, another player, Rob, kept pestering me to buy a ticket. All of a sudden the new blond boy, Chad Stendal, spoke up. "It's no use, Rob," he remarked, "She'll never buy a ticket from you. She's waiting for Bill to invite her to the game."

I almost fainted from shock and rage. How could this stranger read my mind so well? My intention certainly wasn't obvious to anyone else. Bill looked up from his plate, mildly surprised but said nothing. I just wished there were some way I could strangle Chad Stendal.

Later as I was drying dishes in the church kitchen, Chad joined me. Picking up a dishtowel, he clumsily dried the large, heavy restaurant-type plates. "I'm sorry that I embarrassed you out there," he casually remarked. "What I really meant to do was to ask you to go to the basketball game with me." You certainly picked the wrong way of doing it, I thought, but as we finished drying the dishes together, I found myself agreeing to go to the game with him the next Friday night.

To my surprise, the next afternoon I received a telephone call from Bill inviting me to attend the game with him. Obviously, he had never considered asking me for a date until Chad had given him the idea. Thinking it over, or perhaps after being turned down by someone else, he had decided it was not such a bad plan. With consternation I had to explain that I had agreed to go with Chad. I was trying to leave the door open for a future invitation, but I realized from past experience that when a young man was turned down once, he rarely called a second time. Once again I wished I could strangle Chad Stendal.

On Friday evening, Chad picked me up in his jalopy, a 1933 Rockne with a rumble seat. I fell in love with the car at once. As an avid basketball fan, I had always followed all the plays and watched the score closely. To me, basketball was one of the important things of life. However that Friday night, sitting in the gymnasium with Chad, I lost track of the score. I hardly knew which teams were playing. I don't know what we talked about, but whatever it was, it became more interesting than the basketball game. On the way home in the jalopy, Chad invited me to go bicycle-riding with him the next afternoon and also asked me to be his date for the church young people's formal banquet that was coming up in two weeks or so. I accepted both invitations.

After an enjoyable bicycle ride along the Mississippi River, we ended up in Minnehaha Park where Chad produced wieners and proceeded to build a fire. As we relaxed around the campfire, he asked me if I thought his car would make it out to Oxboro the following Saturday. I assured him that I thought it would. Oxboro was an area in suburban Minneapolis where Bethesda had extended a helping hand to a small congregation. Our young people's group went out once a month to lead a youth service as a part of our home missions outreach. All loyal members were expected to participate. We all met at Bethesda, then piled into the cars brought by a few of our members for the trip out to the suburbs, as Oxboro lay beyond the city transit system. As I assured Chad that I believed his car could make the trip, he stated that he would like to have me go in his car the next weekend.

As the week drew to a close, I received another phone call from Bill. He invited me to go to the Sportsman's Show on Saturday night. I was astonished and chagrined. Bill was one of the most faithful leaders of the young people's group. Had he forgotten about our commitment at Oxboro? Timidly, I reminded him. "Of course!" he said, " We'll go to Oxboro. I'll pick you up at 6:45 p.m."

I was horrified to find myself agreeing. How could I turn Bill down a second time? He would never call me again. As I hung up the phone, I had a sickening trapped feeling. I had accepted two dates for the same night, same place. My brain raced for a solution. Surely Chad had not meant to ask me as his date, he had merely asked whether I thought his car would make it and then said I could ride in his car. That must be it. But down inside, I was not so sure. I thought and thought. Suddenly an idea hit me.

When plans had been laid for the formal banquet, committees had been appointed. Bill was the chairman of the publicity committee, and I was the only other member. He had not contacted me in any way regarding publicity for the banquet, doing it all himself, however now in desperation my mind conceived a plan. I found Chad's number in the telephone directory and quickly dialed lest I lose my nerve. "I'm sorry I can't ride in your car to Oxboro on Saturday," I told him. "I have to go to a committee meeting instead." I felt greatly relieved as I hung up the phone. It seemed that I had handled a difficult situation very well.

Saturday evening arrived. Bill picked me up at my home in a sedate looking dark blue sedan. In the back seat was one of the couples from our Young People's group, older members whom I barely knew. The radio was playing; Spike Jones' weekly program was on the air. As I struggled to make conversation, the other three occupants of the car snapped at me. The message was clear. I was to keep quiet. They were listening to Spike Jones. The ride to Oxboro seemed endless. I found Spike Jones to be quite boring, but I didn't dare to open my mouth again. We rode in silence except for the blaring radio. As we arrived at the little chapel, I was looking forward to seeing the other young people but found myself hurried down towards the front with Bill and the other couple. I kept looking around for Chad, wondering if he would have room in his car for me on the way back, but to my dismay, I did not see either him or his car.

Halfway through the service, the door opened, and in walked Chad with a pretty girl who infrequently attended our church. My heart sank as I saw right away that she was his date for the evening. I reconciled myself to a long, boring ride home.

Right after the service Chad rushed over to greet me. "We would have been here on time," he said with a big smile, "But we had to stop and have a committee meeting on the way."

Driving back to the city, the radio was turned off, and some attempt at conversation was made, but I didn't feel like talking. We stopped at a nice little restaurant for refreshments, and my three companions ordered cake and coffee. Since my parents had never allowed me to drink coffee, I ordered cake and milk. The others found this extremely amusing, and my discomfort grew. I was very glad when we arrived at my home.

A dismal depression overwhelmed me. Chad had obviously dropped me for the other girl, and I never wanted to go out with any of the older young people again. What about the formal banquet the next Saturday? I had so looked forward to it and had my dress all ready. I felt sad as I went to church the next morning. As usual Chad sang in the choir. When the choir members took places in the congregation just before the message, Chad sat directly in front of me. At the end of the benediction, he turned around, looked me square in the eye, and said, "Just remember *where* you are going next Saturday night, and *who* you are going with."

Chad and his dad at their lake place in 1948.

Part Two: A Vision is Formed

Pat - 1948.

Chapter 12

On Trial

Minnesota, 1948

As spring slid into summer, the 1933 Rockne was often parked in front of 4440 Bryant Avenue. I had warned Chad about my outspoken father who had scared away other boyfriends. He promised not to be intimidated, and indeed he wasn't, not even when it became evident that Dad had a special dislike for Second Lieutenants — a holdover from his days in the U. S. Navy.

Mother liked Chad from the start, and he was always a welcome guest in our home. As Chad lived east of the church, and I lived far to the west, we had plenty of time to talk as Chad drove me home after church functions in his 1933 Rockne. One evening as we were driving west on 38th Street in a line of bumper-to-bumper traffic, Chad casually remarked, "I would really like to know how you feel about me."

Searching for a tactful but noncommittal answer, I replied in an offhanded way, "Oh, I suppose I feel about you just the same as you feel about me."

"You do!" he exclaimed, turning to look at me, a broad smile covering his face. Crash! The line of traffic had halted, and we banged into the car ahead of us. Crestfallen, as the irate driver of the other car headed for us, Chad turned to me and mumbled, "There's a time and a place for everything." Luckily, the other car was not damaged, and Chad quickly reattached his jalopy's front bumper with a piece of wire.

Sometimes we talked about his army experiences, especially in the South Pacific. He confided to me that he felt he might return someday as a Christian missionary. I imagined myself in a cheery Hawaiian print dress, serving tall, cool glasses of pineapple juice to my missionary husband and his native converts.

Chad planned to attend the summer session at Macalester College, but his friends, Bob and Virginia, an engaged couple who were attending Northwestern Bible Institute were going to northern Minnesota to hold Daily Vacation Bible Schools (DVBS) in rural communities under the auspices of the American Sunday School Union. Bob had lined up a young man to accompany him, but Virginia needed a female partner. Chad presented the need to me and gave me a low-key suggestion that perhaps this would be a good way for me to spend my summer. I jumped at the chance, little realizing that Chad had set it all up as an evaluating experience for me, to see if I could stand up under difficult circumstances before formally asking me to marry him. Bob and Virginia were to report back to him, especially concerning my reaction under pressure and to tough living conditions. He didn't want to get saddled with a wimpy city girl who demanded an easy life.

In early June, six or eight of us young people congregated at the rural missionaries' home just outside of Grand Rapids, Minnesota. On Sunday afternoon, we were taken two by two to the areas where we would be holding DVBS. The American Sunday School Union had organized Sunday Schools in rural communities, usually in the town hall, and we were to hold intensive one or two week Bible teaching classes for the children, followed by a closing program for the entire community. The local parents were responsible for housing and feeding us. Usually we slept and had breakfast in one home, and our hostess arranged a schedule for lunch and dinner in the homes of the other children. Our first assignment was at Blackberry, a small community just east of Grand Rapids. This was a one-week school with sessions both morning and afternoon. I can still remember the warm, freshly baked bread, fried chicken, creamed green peas with new potatoes, and corn-on-the-cob. The mothers vied with one another to entertain us itinerant teachers royally.

Most communities opted for a two-week school of morning classes, giving us free afternoons to prepare lessons, play with the children, and visit the members of the community. With our first school being a one-weeker, Virginia and I were very busy until late at night, cutting out our flannel-graph figures to illustrate the stories and preparing the lessons. I was also the piano player, so I had to learn to play the choruses that Virginia would be teaching the children. I scrawled a few hastily scribbled notes to Chad but was embarrassed at my feeble literary attempt when his frequent letters started showing up. They were masterpieces of literary expression and penmanship. (His mother later told me that he sat up most of the night composing them.) Somehow a beautiful flowering plant also arrived from Chad that week, so I set it on the dresser of

This is the picture of Chad in his US Army uniform that I carried with me all summer in Grand Rapids, MN.

our farmhouse bedroom beside the large picture that he had given me of himself in army uniform.

Virginia was a talented teacher and Bible school director. She seemed to know just what to do, so I followed her lead, and soon we were conducting very successful classes. I found that my many years of Bible study had prepared me more than I had ever imagined. It was a thrill to pass on to the children some of the information that had been stored in my head by reading the Bible and other Christian books and the teaching I had received in my home, church, and school.

On the weekends between schools, we teachers stayed at the home of the Sunday School Union missionaries, Mr. & Mrs. Sandberg and their five young children. These missionaries were living on a very low income, and Mrs. Sandberg was hard pressed to feed all of us teenagers as well as her growing family. I was a very finicky eater with a particular dislike for eggs and a revulsion for unpasteurized milk as I had been warned in school of the health hazards entailed. On one of these weekends a neighbor sent over several loaves of home baked bread, and another sent several dozen eggs fresh from her chickens. I was very disappointed to find at lunchtime that the eggs had been fried and served between slices of bread as sandwiches, but my hunger prevailed, and with the first bite, my prejudice against fried eggs was gone forever.

On another weekend, Mrs. Sandberg was wringing her hands in despair as her husband had taken all the boys to town and was late in arriving to milk the goat. She had counted on the goat's milk for supper, and now had nothing to feed six hungry teen-agers and her own five children. About five o'clock, I suggested that maybe I could milk the goat. The closest I had been to milking was that I had once watched a man milk a cow, but I was getting very hungry, so I assured the woman that I could do it. Virginia held the animal's head, and one of the little girls held the hind legs. With a great deal of effort, I was able to extract a large bowl of milk. Our hostess was elated. She immediately started preparations for chipped beef gravy. However, the family cat, who was also hungry, leaped onto the table, knocked over the bowl and happily started lapping it up off the floor. The lady was dismayed. I thought she was going to cry. I quickly picked up the bowl and calling the girls went back to the goat. We succeeded in filling the bowl again, finishing just as the missionary turned into the driveway.

Our last school was quite different from the others. It was held in the town hall of a small community south of Grand Rapids, right in front of a ballpark. The American Sunday School missionary had not yet succeeded in establishing a Sunday School in this community, but one farm family was very interested in the DVBS. Mr. Sandberg thought that having the vacation Bible school there might open the door to a weekly Sunday School. The one family was very supportive, but the other families were not too eager to become involved. The friendly woman said that we could sleep on army cots in the town hall kitchen and do our own cooking. She sent a quart of milk, fresh from the cow, every morning with her son who seemed to be somewhat retarded. The boy, a painfully shy lad, looked the other way as he handed me the quart jar of milk but still somehow made me understand that I must empty it immediately as he had to return the jar to his mother. Not knowing what to do with the milk, I quickly dumped it into a huge coffee pot and shoved the coffee pot under my army cot. Virginia and I were both city girls, and we had been taught the dangers of drinking unpasteurized milk. We had no idea what to do with this milk that came every day, so every morning I pulled out the coffee pot, dumped in another quart, and shoved it back under the bed again.

Eventually the other families started inviting us out to eat, and on Thursday evening, when we returned to the town hall after supper, the lights were on, and a small crowd had gathered. No one had told us it was the night for the community town meeting. Several women were frantically searching the kitchen for the large coffee pot. While Virginia engaged them in small-talk, I sneaked the coffee pot out from under my cot and into the back yard. Quickly I dumped the milk on the ground, but to my surprise it had turned to curds and whey. While the liquid soaked into the ground, a huge mound of white curd sat on the ground, silently testifying to the whole community of our finickiness and wastefulness. As I stood there mortified, not knowing what to do, a huge Black Labrador dog came bounding around the corner and gobbled the evidence all up in one gulp.

I quickly rinsed out the coffee pot under the stream of water from the hand pump in the yard and got it into the hands of the refreshment committee. One woman kept complaining that the coffee just didn't have the same good flavor that it usually had when cooked in that pot, but the general public didn't seem to mind.

At the end of the week, Chad drove up to Grand Rapids in his strange Rockne. For some reason the gas stations were all closed, but he made it by draining the last drops out of all the gas pumps he passed. I must have received a good report from Bob and Virginia, because he took me out to a bench in the deserted ballpark and asked me to marry him.

Chapter 13

Enduring Hardness

Early in the spring of 1948, as my year at Augsburg drew to a close, I once again tried to persuade Dad to let me attend a Christian college as a boarding student, even offering to earn my own expenses above what he was already paying. Dad flatly turned this idea down. He wanted me at home — under his roof and watchful care.

While Chad was visiting me in northern Minnesota, he suggested that we both enroll at Northwestern Bible Institute (later college) in Minneapolis for one semester. As a fairly new convert, Chad felt that this would give him a good foundation for his Christian life and strengthen his faith for his later studies in civil engineering at the University of Minnesota. Since engineering was a five-year program, he did not feel that he could devote more than one semester to study at the Bible Institute. Northwestern was an institution of great reputation in the area, connected with the very large First Baptist Church in downtown Minneapolis. Dr. W.B. Riley was the renowned pastor, although now in decline due to age and health, and Billy Graham (of Youth for Christ fame before his great success as an evangelist) was president of the Bible Institute.

I agreed with his suggestion and decided not to return to Augsburg, but to enroll with Chad as a special student at

Northwestern. This meant that we could take any courses that appealed to us without regard to grade level or prerequisites. Then we would both start the University of Minnesota at midyear.

Leaving me to counsel at a summer camp for the DVBS children, Chad hurried back to Minneapolis. He had already signed up for a two-week tour of active duty teaching basic training to new recruits in California. As a Second Lieutenant, his pay would be better than at any other temporary summer job, and in addition, he was to receive six cents a mile travel pay between Minneapolis and California. He and a friend were planning to hitchhike and save the travel money.

After camp I returned to Minneapolis where my family proudly welcomed me home. Dad was not pleased, however, with my decision to go to Northwestern. He did not believe we really would go to the University of Minnesota later, and he was afraid I would be diverted from earning the college degree that meant so much to him. I had never told Dad that the degree program I had enrolled in at Augsburg was to qualify me to be a high school physical education teacher. He would not have been pleased, nor would I have been a success at that career. I didn't know that then of course. When I enrolled at Augsburg, I was trying to play the role of an active, athletic, sports-minded extrovert.

Soon a letter arrived from California. Chad and his friend had had trouble getting rides as hitchhikers, so they had decided to buy three-speed racing bikes (a new idea in those days) and bicycle back to Minnesota. He informed me that with the rest of his money, he was buying me a 1/2-carat diamond engagement ring and a wedding band at the U. S. Army Post Exchange where he could get a very good deal. I was shocked at this news! Things were going entirely too fast as far as I was concerned. I had more or less accepted Chad's proposal of marriage, but to me this was far off in the future. Now, the idea of something as concrete as a diamond ring sent me into a panic. Laboriously, I composed a ten-page letter, explaining why I didn't want to accept a diamond ring yet. I ended up by saying I felt too young and inexperienced to commit myself so definitely. Besides, I was still terrified of Dad and was sure he would have a fit if I even mentioned engagement and marriage. After writing the letter, the thought came to me that in something so important as marriage, I should really ask God about it. If I sent the letter as it was, I might lose Chad altogether. I really didn't want that to happen; I just wanted to postpone a serious commitment for a while. I got down on my knees by my bed and asked the Lord if I had done the right thing. After awhile I really felt that I should not send the letter as it was. Too exhausted to rewrite the entire letter, I tore up only the last page and replaced it with a new one. "Go ahead and buy the ring, since you can get such a good bargain," I wrote, "Even though I don't want to wear it now, I probably will later on."

Several weeks later, Chad telephoned me from Iowa. He and his friend were bucking a head wind and were terribly tired but hoped to arrive in Minneapolis sometime the next day. He had bought the ring. He had read through the entire nine pages, anticipating that I was turning him down. The surprise ending had left him bewildered, but he had bought the beautiful solitaire and had it with him, and was reconciled to the fact that I would not be wearing it right away. I told him that I was very worried about him and insisted that he call me as soon as he had arrived safely in Minneapolis.

At 2:00 a.m., the telephone rang. I lost the race to the phone, and Dad answered. "What do you mean by calling my daughter at this hour?" he roared. Somehow I got the receiver away from him, and he went back to bed. Chad had arrived and would meet me at church the next morning, which was Sunday.

We invited him home for dinner after church. He was terribly thin but nicely suntanned, and his leg muscles were like iron. He had eaten five meals a day and lost twenty pounds in the two weeks of biking across the United States. When Dad at last understood what Chad had done, he scolded me for not keeping him properly informed. This was the kind of physical feat he admired. "Why, if I had known what you had done," he smiled, patting Chad on the back, "I'd have been out to meet you with a band, not bawling you out on the phone."

Our semester at Northwestern occurred during the short period of Billy Graham's presidency and also the birth of radio station KTIS, one of the very first Christian radio stations, certainly the first in the Midwest. Shortly before, there was a threat of removing all Christian programs from commercial stations, so Christians had joined forces to put a Christian station on the air. It would be housed and centered at Northwestern Bible Institute. At one point in late 1948, everything was ready to launch the station onto the airwaves except there was no cash for daily operating expenses. Billy Graham earnestly brought this need before the assembled student body of Northwestern at one of our daily chapel meetings. We as Bible school students were certainly not the most likely source of funds, but we were told that one dollar a week from each of us would be enough to put the station on the air. We eagerly pledged our support. I was determined to pay this pledge myself and not take money from Dad, so I found a part time job selling children's clothing in a downtown department store.

One chilly gray November day, Chad invited me to lunch at our favorite Chinese restaurant. Over a plate of chow mein and steaming cups of Chinese tea, he informed me that he had signed up to go into the army again for a two month paratrooper and glider school. He was elated that in addition to his lieutenant's salary and travel pay, this time he would receive an additional compensation for hazardous duty. I was very upset. I had accepted his diamond ring some two weeks before on his 21st birthday, and so we were now officially engaged. Although a notice appeared in the church bulletin commenting that the Young People now did not need electric lights, since Pat Carlson was wearing Chad Stendal's engagement ring. (A 1/2 caret diamond was a huge stone in our circle of friends in those days.) Dad had not seemed to notice. Mother was pleased. She had always liked Chad.

One of Dad's strong, often repeated opinions was that jumping out of airplanes was a foolish risk of life and limb. One of his coworkers had a son who had volunteered for parachute training during the war. On his first jump, he had permanently damaged his ankle and now received disability payments. Dad saw himself as a protector and guardian of government funds and property, primarily in his capacity as superintendent of the Minneapolis Post Office building, but also in general areas. One of his repeated dinnertime monologues concerned this "nincompoop" who thought it would be a great adventure to parachute and now was a lifelong disability problem for the government, his family, and himself.

As Chad told me his plans, tears started falling on my chow mein noodles. I really wanted Chad to be liked and accepted by my dad. How could I go home and tell him that Chad had now classed himself with the nincompoop? Chad tried to console me by telling me that this time he would save the money he earned and put it into a savings account towards our marriage. He thought that we should have a thousand dollars in the bank in order to start married life in a responsible manner. To me, however, his present companionship was more important than future marriage plans.

In spite of my tears, on November 22, a few days before Thanksgiving, I bade Chad farewell at the Minneapolis Bus Station. I had been too young to have a soldier boyfriend during World War II, but now I felt quite grownup as Chad in his smart-looking officer's uniform stepped through the exit to the waiting Greyhound bus. My eyes were blurred by tears, as I left the station alone, walking through lightly falling flakes of snow to the trolley car where I sat miserably, dreading to tell my family what had happened. That evening at the dinner table, my worst fears were realized. The story of the nincompoop was related again, and Dad was sure that he now knew two of them.

The month passed quickly. I decided if Chad was brave enough to jump out of airplanes, I should be able to get my tonsils out. I had been putting this off since I was nine years old and was subject to frequent respiratory infections and sore throats each winter. I surprised my family by getting an appointment with my aunt's family doctor and having my tonsils removed under local anesthetic in his office. I continued to work at the department store until Christmas Eve and kept my commitment to KTIS. In addition, with the generous discount given by the department store to their employees, I was able to buy gifts for my family as well as a beautiful royal blue coat with a gray fur collar and cuffs in the long, "new look" style, as well as two lovely dresses, one black velvet, and the other royal blue satin. I felt healthy, brave, and attractive when Chad arrived on military leave on Christmas Eve.

On New Year's Eve, we attended a "watch night" service at River Lake Tabernacle, the church that Chad had attended before he was drafted. As was his custom, the pastor spent several hours reviewing the past year in the light of Bible prophecy. It had been quite a year. The nation of Israel had been born among other important happenings. As the old year went out and the new came in, Chad and I were down on our knees, committing our lives as a couple to the Lord for whatever He willed for us. We were sure the time was very short until the rapture.

All too soon, Chad boarded the bus again for Fort Benning, Georgia, for one more month of training. This time I was not quite so devastated.

Chapter 14

Adversities

In early January, bundled up in a heavy winter coat and knee socks, I braved the windswept campus of the University of Minnesota and enrolled. Here I was given a battery of tests and once again was required to choose a life occupation. Dad and I had more or less agreed on the teaching profession, but *who* and *what* did I want to teach?

On the basis of the test results, consideration of my personal interest, and job availability, the decision was made. I would major in elementary education with an emphasis on grades four through six. My minor would be the social sciences. My credits from Augsburg transferred over very favorably, and to my great relief, the University of Minnesota College of Education had no language requirement for graduation. (So much for Greek.)

Chad returned at the end of the month in time to register for the spring semester at Macalester. He would not transfer to the University until the summer session. True to his word, he opened a savings account and announced that when the balance showed $1,000 dollars, we would get married. The first time he came to dinner after his return, he so entertained my dad with tales from his parachuting experiences that Dad forgot all about his prejudices and the other young jumper. For years he recounted the parachute adventures of his future son-in-law to his coworkers and friends.

Upon returning from California, Chad sold his 1933 Rockne and bought a second racing bicycle, which he loaned to me. We made several short trips together, and I often rode across the city of Minneapolis on my bicycle to the University campus. I could make the trip in less than an hour, less time than it took to take the bus downtown and transfer to one that would take me to the University. One drizzly October morning, I left home a bit late. I almost decided to take the bus because of the rain, but then decided I had a better chance of making my first class on time by taking the bicycle. Speeding down 38th Street, a traffic light flashed yellow in front of me. Picking up speed, I intended to beat the light, but noticing the line-up of cars ready to take off in the rush hour traffic, I chickened out and touched the front wheel brake.

The bicycle reacted as though it had suddenly become a bucking bronco. I was thrown over the handlebars into the intersection. I got up but found that my left leg would not hold my weight. I hopped to the side of the street and sat on the curb while a kindly old man retrieved my bicycle. After a while a motorist stopped, drove me home, and carried me into the house. At noon, Mother returned home and took me at once to the University hospital where X-rays revealed a rather freakish injury. A small bone in my knee, called the spine of the tibia, had broken off and was pulled up into my knee by the attached ligament. Surgery was necessary, and for months I walked with a stiff leg. Physical therapy restored some of the motion, and by continuing the treatments at home, I was finally able to bend it enough to sit in a bus seat.

While I was in the hospital, Chad decided that I would not be bicycling for a while. He had previously bought a small English motorcycle, but now he purchased a Triumph 500 Speed Twin, which he brought to the curb outside my hospital window to show me. Unfortunately, my father was visiting me at the time. "He has already crippled my daughter! Now he intends to kill her!" he shouted. Dad was especially upset by my accident. He was now paying tuition at Minnehaha Academy for Dorothe, as well as my tuition at the University. Not only was the accident an extra expense that he didn't need, but it brought back memories of his mother losing her leg after an accident. Gangrene had set in under her cast, leading to the amputation of her leg. Now, seeing me with my leg in a cast caused him to worry that the same thing would happen to me. And in his eyes, it was all Chad Stendal's fault. He was convinced that I would never have gotten into riding English racing bicycles, much less motorcycles, if it weren't for him.

If it took my father a while to get used to his future son-in-law, it took Jean and Russell Stendal even longer to get used to me. The Stendals had been completely unprepared for Chad's dramatic conversion to Christianity shortly before his induction into the U. S. Army. Chad had been a difficult teenager but had graduated from St. Thomas Military academy and had shown talent at the piano. Russell had hoped that his son would use his musical ability entertaining in nightclubs, accompanying his father who played the violin, and was extremely disappointed in this new turn of events. Jean remembered that she had committed Chad to God before he was born, and Grandmother Thea wrote him encouraging letters from Norway that Jean dutifully translated into English. However both Russell and Jean were hoping that he would marry a girl who would lead him back into the social life that they enjoyed so much.

It took time to accumulate money in the savings account, but by the spring of 1950 the balance passed the $900. dollar mark, and we started to make wedding plans. On June 10th we were married at the Bethesda church. Our wedding was scheduled for 7:30 p.m. on a Saturday evening. Another couple from the church was married at 4:00 p.m. the same day. Since Mother and I decided to spend my savings account (money that had accumulated in the bank since

I was born) on my wedding reception, we had hired a caterer. She came to our house six weeks or so before the wedding, and we ordered from the catalog of lovely pictures that she showed us: a beautiful cake with a bride and groom on top (the bride's dress was surprisingly similar to mine) pastel ice cream balls, and lovely delicate china with tiny blossoms around the borders. Since I would not be using any of the church dishes, the other bride, who was having her reception in a home, sorted through the heavy, white restaurant-style plates in the kitchen and took the ones without chips or cracks.

After our lovely wedding ceremony we knelt at the altar while a soloist sang,

Savior, like a shepherd lead us,
Much we need Thy tender care,
In Thy pleasant pastures feed us,
For our use Thy folds prepare:

Blessed Jesus, blessed Jesus,
You have bought us Thine we are; . . .

We are Thine; do Thou befriend us,
Be the Guardian of our way;
Keep Thy flock, from sin defend us,
Seek us when we go astray:

Blessed Jesus, blessed Jesus,
Hear, O hear us when we pray; . . .

Early let us seek Thy favor,
Early let us do Thy will.
Blessed Lord and only Savior,
With Thy love our bosoms fill.

Blessed Jesus, blessed Jesus,
Thou hast loved us, love us still; . . .

Our wedding at Bethesda Church.

My brother, Darrell, greets me in the reception line Dorothe, Chad, Pat, Dick Carlson, Jean and Russell Stendal.

108 Minnesota Mom in the Land of the Ancient Mother
Part Two: A Vision is Formed

June 10, 1950.

My mother, me, Chad's mother.

Then we were hustled down to the basement to cut the first piece of cake. I noticed that the cake was not what I had ordered. This one was much smaller and had a bell on top. The caterer was nowhere to be seen, but two nervous young girls were scurrying around. With some difficulty, an ordinary table knife was found to cut the cake. We were then hurried back upstairs to the sanctuary to pose for the photographer while our wedding guests were being served.

When at last we returned to the church parlors in the basement, I realized vaguely as though seeing through a fog that something was wrong. Pink, green, and yellow balls of ice cream were rolling around on the floor. Some men had put their ice cream balls in their coffee in an effort to soften them, and steam was arising out of their cups. The inexperienced girls had not known that the ice cream balls should have been removed from the dry ice in advance. Since no china had arrived, the girls had gotten out the church plates, the cracked and chipped ones. The disorder barely registered in my subconscience and didn't bother me at all. We sat in a circle with our wedding attendants and ate our refreshments. Then I changed to my going away suit, and amidst a shower of rice, we entered my family's car that Dad was loaning us for the occasion. We drove around the block where Chad got rid of the tin cans, etc. Somehow we ditched the driver, Chad's best man, and headed for the Stendal family's lake cabin for our honeymoon.

Several days later, I called my mother and found her all upset about the wedding reception. She told me that the caterer had accepted a number of receptions that Saturday evening in June. The deliveries had been confused. My order had gone elsewhere, and someone else's had come to me. My mother in her nervous confusion the night of the reception had signed a paper saying that everything was fine before she realized all the things that had gone wrong, so we never were able to get any of the money back. Anyway, some unsuspecting couple got a big beautiful cake and special china that they didn't order.

Part Two: A Vision is Formed

Pat and Chad leave the church
amid a shower of rice after the ceremony.

Off to the Stendal's lake cabin in my parents' car.

Chapter 15

I Married Adventure

By now Chad was enrolled in the University of Minnesota, and we secured a small house trailer in University Village, a trailer park run by the university to serve married ex- G.I.'s. There was no running water, but hot and cold water came out of a faucet at the main building. Fuel oil came out of another. The monthly charge that included everything, even electricity, was $25.00. I had been worried about my homemaking skills. I was basically a bookish, student type, not too interested in housekeeping. After Grandma Winburn's death, I had taken over the job of baking goodies for the family, but that was about all I knew about household responsibilities. We had $105.00 a month to live on, Chad's income under the G. I. Bill of Rights as a student. We fixed up the little house trailer and really fell in love with it. We replaced the icebox with a small electric refrigerator, and covered the floor with new linoleum. We wished it were ours and that it were still on wheels so that we could take it with us and keep it forever.

I enrolled in summer school at the university and Dad obligingly paid my tuition as he always had. After my first week of classes, to my surprise I was offered a summer job as a playground director by the Minneapolis Park Board. I canceled out of my classes and received a refund that I intended to use for my tuition for the fall quarter. It was a little hard for me to get to my job at the playground, as I had to use Chad's small motorcycle, The Famous James. Chad used the larger one, The Triumph Speed Twin, to go to his classes at the University. The Famous James was a hard starter. Chad could get me going in the morning, but I often had trouble getting it started when it was time to come home in the afternoon. We began to feel the need for an automobile. The almost $1,000.00 in our joint account that had seemed like a fortune in June had dwindled down, but there was still enough for a car. Chad picked out a 1937 Chrysler. It was still in the old prewar style, black with straight perpendicular lines. It reminded me of my family's early cars in which I rode coast to coast when Dad installed elevators for Westinghouse. It took the last cent we had in the bank, but we were so pleased with it. We proudly drove it over to show Dad. To our horror, it stalled on the streetcar tracks in front of 4440 Bryant. Dad came out and helped us push it off the track, then he checked it over thoroughly and pronounced it to have a rod knock, one of the worst defects a used car could have. Some kind of heavy oil had been put in the engine so the potential buyer would not detect the rod knock until the deal was closed. Dad tried to no avail to get our money back, so he did the next best thing — he fixed it up. The car gave us nine or ten months of good service.

Chad and I were still troubled by the fact that we were "throwing away" $25 per month on the rent at University Village. Soon after buying the car we took a trip to Chicago with my dad to look for a used house trailer. In those days we thought Chicago was the place to go to find a good deal on used vehicles. Dad entertained us by telling us of his previous trips to Chicago. One time the car he and his father were driving lost all its oil right on one of the main streets of Chicago. To add to their troubles, a policeman came over to bawl them out for the terrible mess they had made on the street. My grandfather, who was evidently even more hot-tempered than my father, started to roar at him, "Well, if you don't like it—" then in mid sentence, realizing it was the law he was talking to, tamely finished, "we'll have to clean it up." That struck Dad as very funny, and he roared with laughter.

After looking through a couple of used trailer lots, I found my dream trailer. It was dark blue on the outside and on the inside had all the necessary appliances and furniture, but the feature that really caught my eye was that the table served double duty as the door for the dish cupboard. You just pulled down the table, standing it on the leg that folded out, and there were your dishes, right handy to your table. Dad says I just sat there on the sofa like I was never going to leave without buying that house trailer. There was no sensible way we could do it. Our money in the bank was gone, and Chad's income was just $105.00 a month. In my desperation, I thought of a plan. Mother had an elderly lady friend, who was known to be quite wealthy. I would ask her for a loan.

We drove until late in the night to get back to Minneapolis, but before I went to bed, I told Mother about the loan I needed from Miss Twine. When I woke up late the next morning, Mother told me with a big smile that the answer was yes. Miss Twine would loan us the money. The terms of repayment would be $100.00 per month.

Chad was scheduled to attend a mountain warfare-training course in Colorado Springs, Colorado, so he and I took off on the Triumph Speed twin with a big duffel bag of camping gear tied on the package rack. There was just enough room for me to squeeze in between Chad and the duffle bag. Mother contacted a sister of Grandma Winburn's who lived in Colorado Springs, and made arrangements for us to stay with her while Chad took the two-week course.

Chad and I had a memorable trip to Colorado. I had not been west since I was old enough to really remember. I enjoyed the rolling plains of South Dakota and the colorful badlands. Chad had taken the same trip alone the year before on the Famous James. He assured me that he slept very comfortably in haystacks along the way. The first night we had trouble finding a suitable haystack. At last we saw one some distance from the road. When we got over to it, we found it was very old, and the hay was moldy and stuck to the haystack. We managed to pull out enough to cushion our sleeping bags, but I spent a miserable cold night while Chad slept soundly. I'm sure the sleeping bag I borrowed from my brother was not as warm as his. I spent the last few hours with my back huddled into the haystack, facing east, waiting for the sunrise so that I could wake Chad up, and we could get on our way again. Later that day, I found that food on this trip consisted of canned pork and beans that Chad heated on an open fire. He knew just when to take the can out of the fire. Then he opened it, and we ate it with two spoons that he carried in the motorcycle saddlebags. I soon burned both of my ankles on the twin exhausts, and when I started burning them again on top of the burns, Chad stopped at an army surplus store and bought me a pair of combat boots. That took care of my ankles, but then my nose started to sunburn. We stopped at another place and got me a headgear that consisted of a bubble mask and a black headscarf with a visor. Since my nose was still out in the sun, I started wearing the bubble mask upside down with a wad of Kleenex under the nose to give me a breathing hole. I really looked like something from

Our trip to Colorado. Chad sat in front of me on the Triumph Speed Twin in the driver's seat.

outer space. Later a pair of fatigue army pants was added to my costume.

We arrived at the Colorado Springs army post late one evening. We felt it was too late to bother my great-aunt Dolly, so we went right to the army camp. Chad knew they would give him a place to sleep in the officers' quarters, but he didn't know what to do with me. Chad stopped to put on his gold 2nd lieutenant bar, his army engineers' castle, and his jump wings before approaching the guard tower. I was completely taken by surprise when the guards snapped to attention and saluted Chad, their hands encased in spotless white gloves. I started to giggle thinking it was some kind of joke. Chad spoke to the soldier in charge, a sergeant, and asked if there was a guesthouse or somewhere where I could spend the night. "Why she can just go right over to my house and spend the night with my wife," he responded with a southern drawl. "I have to work all night, so there is plenty of room."

We were directed to the sergeant's house where the wife gave us something to eat, and then let me share her double bed, while Chad went to the officers' quarters. The next morning Chad picked me up and we went into the town of Colorado Springs to find Aunt Dolly's house. I was awestruck by the majestic beauty of the mountains around Colorado Springs. In reality, it was much more beautiful than I had ever imagined from pictures. I had always been told that Minnesota with all its lakes was the most beautiful state in the union, however now I felt it really lacked something — a few mountains.

We found Aunt Dolly in a white frame two-story house. She looked just like a younger version of my beloved Grandma Winburn. Although almost blind, she rented out rooms to make ends meet. Mother had written to her about our coming, but she had misunderstood and thought that we were moving to Colorado Springs permanently. She had thought that I would be a big help in running the rooming house and was sorely disappointed to hear that we were only staying two weeks. Soon we were installed in one of the upstairs back bedrooms. Chad had told me about the officers' club and warned me that I must dress appropriately and use my best manners. I had mailed two dresses to myself via General Delivery, so we went to the post office to pick them up, and I changed in a restroom somewhere. Following this quick change of clothes, we went to lunch at the officers' club. Once again all the saluting at the gate impressed me, and I determined to make a good impression and not embarrass Chad at the club. I had been seeing signs advertising rainbow trout all along the road, so I was delighted to find it on the menu, even though I didn't normally like fish. I wanted to try this exotic delicacy found in this fascinating area. Of course I assumed it would be filleted. Suddenly Chad leaned over and cautioned me to get a grip on myself and not make a scene. He could see what I could not as yet — a waiter coming towards me with an entire rainbow trout on a plate, head, tail, eyes, fins and all. When this was set before me, it was all I could do to keep from jumping up from the table and screaming; however Chad continued looking at me very sternly saying, "You ordered it! You have to eat it!" I was sure I could never take a mouthful, but I finally solved the problem. I took the skin off with my fork and covered the head and tail. This exposed white meat underneath which I picked at until Chad was satisfied. I learned my lesson! I have never made that mistake again.

The next morning, dressed in my army clothes, I accompanied Chad to report in for duty. A number of other wives, some with children, had come with their husbands, but I was the only one on a motorcycle. In 1950 women still did not wear pants very often, and the others were all nicely dressed in colorful dresses. The men were all loaded onto huge army trucks and driven out to the mountain training area. The women and children swung into line behind the army trucks. I had a big problem. I couldn't get the motorcycle started. I jumped on the starter and jumped on the starter, but it just wouldn't start. Just as the last car was pulling out, the friendly sergeant appeared. When I explained my problem, he easily started the motorcycle, and I swung into line behind the last car.

When we arrived at the training area, I parked the Triumph and found Chad's group. He was delighted that his instructor was the Swiss Hans Wagner, the same as he had had last year. As Chad's group of some ten soldiers led by Hans Wagner filed up the mountainside, I followed along at the rear. The other women and children stayed down on the highway, watching from below. I was doing quite well and had gained quite a bit of altitude, when I discovered to my dismay that the purpose of this climb was to repel down. Repelling consisted of wrapping a long climbing rope around yourself, backing off the cliff into space, controlling your speed by letting out more rope, and keeping yourself off of the rock face of the cliff by kicking with your feet. This was very easy once you got the hang of it, but to a novice like me, it seemed terrifying. I went into a panic and froze to the point that I couldn't even get down the mountain again the way I had come up. Hans Wagner had to excuse Chad and a friend, and they helped me down the steep trail, using their short ropes that every soldier carried. Most of the way down, I slid on the seat of my pants, a most undignified descent in full view of all the soldiers scattered along the mountainsides and the women and children below.

Chad had noticed me climbing up and would have been so proud of me had I been able to repel down like the soldiers. As it was, he was very disappointed and disgusted. He was starting to realize that the outdoors, athletic girl that he thought he had married was really a bookish couch potato.

After Chad and his friend joined their group again, I sat dejectedly by the motorcycle in my army clothes. All of a sudden a car of tourists stopped, a woman jumped out and took a picture of me, then jumped back in the car and sped away again. That made me feel worse. What did they think I was? What would they tell their friends about me when they showed the picture back home? I started to feel hungry. I remembered seeing a tourist restaurant up the road a ways. I managed to start the motorcycle and get myself to the restaurant. It was an excellent restaurant, and I was just finishing a delicious ham and pineapple sandwich when a startling thought hit me. I had not a cent of money. I was sure I would be spending the rest of the day washing dishes, but I bravely approached the cashier and told her my problem. She kindly told me it was okay and to just run along.

The next day I again followed the army trucks to the mountains, but this time I stayed on the road with the other women. I didn't dare go back to that restaurant, even though Chad had given me some money, I was too timid. So at lunchtime, Chad shared his army rations with me. After that I spent my days with Aunt Dolly. She loved to play canasta. I never had had anything to do with playing cards before, but it meant so much to her that I let her teach me. She could just barely see enough to distinguish the cards. I tried timidly to witness to her, but she made it clear that she didn't want to talk about anything spiritual.

During the second week of the training, the men were taken high up into the mountains to learn to climb in ice and snow. Chad took me to the army post exchange store, and it was there I became acquainted with the wife of a captain. She would also be left alone for the week, so she suggested that she and I get together to do some sightseeing. I thought that was a great idea, and we arranged for her to pick me up at Aunt Dolly's house a little later that morning. After the men left, when I tried to get the motorcycle started, I had the same problem again, it wouldn't start. Once again the friendly sergeant appeared out of nowhere. He realized that Chad was gone and wouldn't return until the end of the week. He told me that his wife was also going to be gone that week and invited me to stay with him at his house. I was shocked to the core. I didn't know that real people did things like that. When I told him, " no way," he became very angry. "I suppose a lieutenant's wife feels too good for a sergeant," he muttered. By that time he had the Triumph running, and I beat a hasty retreat and made sure to stay out of his way for the rest of the week.

Back at Aunt Dolly's rooming house, I left the Triumph in the yard and ran upstairs to get ready to go sightseeing. As I came out of the bathroom, there stood one of the other roomers, completely naked. I rushed past him down the stairs where the captain's wife was waiting in her car. We talked the whole thing over and decided that I should not tell Aunt Dolly. She was having enough trouble anyway and probably needed the rent that the man was paying. In the late afternoon when my friend brought me home, I was horrified to find that the same man who had exposed himself was moving from a front bedroom to the other back bedroom, right next to mine. I was really very scared. It seemed too much of a coincidence, but I still didn't feel right about telling Aunt Dolly.

After playing canasta again with Aunt Dolly, I went up to my bedroom. The man was all settled into his new room, and it seemed like there were just the two of us on the second floor. I locked my door and pushed a heavy dresser against it. I was tired, scared, and lonely. I found a used garment of Chad's and put it under my pillow. This gave me a sense of his presence and protection. I finally drifted off into a troubled sleep.

The next morning I went out sightseeing with the captain's wife again. When I told her about the man changing rooms, she decided it was not safe for me to stay there and invited me to spend the rest of the week with her in a nearby motel. I was glad to escape. I told Aunt Dolly I would be spending the rest of the week with a friend, gathered my few belongings, and moved to the motel. The first night my new friend wanted to go to a movie. I had never been to a movie theater in all my life. I thought the devil lived in the theater. I made it clear that I didn't want to go to a movie, so my friend took me to the Greyhound races instead. I was quite amused by the dog races, especially by the little artificial rabbit that ran around the outside of the track, pacing the dogs. We didn't do any betting, but we went to the Greyhound track every night until the men came home. It seemed the lesser of the evils I had been exposed to these last few days.

Even though this trip had been the super economy version, by this time we had spent all my tuition refund and most of the money I had earned at the playground. However when Chad returned, from the last week of the training school, he had some $300.00 in his pocket. He was very tempted to blow it all on a bigger, faster motorcycle (a Vincent Black Shadow that went 125 miles per hour) but I had a fit, and he gave up that idea. We bade Aunt Dolly goodbye and started back to Minneapolis by way of Yellowstone National Park. The first day out, Chad decided that we should climb a 10,000-foot peak. I had never been so tired as on that climb. The altitude seemed to be affecting me. When I couldn't go any farther I would sit down and invariably fall over onto my back. To get me going again, Chad would give me a sip of cherry cider that we had bought along the road. I'm sure that Chad was plenty disgusted with me on that climb, but when at last we reached the top, I was delighted. The view was magnificent with a panorama of peaks in all directions. A stake marked the summit, and under the stake was a can containing a book from the Colorado mountain climbers club. Only two names were entered, so we signed our names as numbers three and four to have climbed that peak. We camped out at 7,000 ft. and spent a shivery night, but the next day we reached Yellowstone.

Here I enjoyed seeing Old Faithful, the Paint Pots, and other phenomena of nature that I had heard about all my life and vaguely remembered seeing on our travels from coast to coast when I was very young. For some reason, at the

Yellowstone campground, Chad decided to put up the tent we had carried with us in the bottom of the duffel bag. Not finding two trees placed exactly right, he hitched one end to the motorcycle. In the early morning hours, the tent collapsed on top of us, and when we were able to extract our heads to see what had happened, we found that a big, black bear had knocked over the motorcycle. He was now about fifty feet away under an electric light examining the contents of our duffle bag. He had already eaten everything edible and soon left, leaving our poor duffle bag with a number of bear claw slashes. He had even made a hole in the toothpaste tube and squeezed out and eaten all the toothpaste.

We packed everything up again, and the next night we camped just outside of Gillette, Wyoming. We spent a comfortable night in a new, fresh haystack, and when we woke up in the morning, we found ourselves surrounded by a semicircle of antelope waiting for us to leave so they could have their breakfast at the haystack. "I would love to come back here during hunting season," Chad commented. A few minutes later when we rode into town, we found it **was** hunting season. A large banner above the street said "Welcome Hunters." Details were given for an antelope-hunting contest that was then in progress.

Big time hunting fever took possession of Chad. He entered the nearest hardware store and found just the right gun that could be bought with the money he had in his pocket. I was aghast. I wanted to get home with that money. I needed to pay my tuition at the university, to say nothing about the debt we had just incurred with the house trailer purchase. I had thrown my weight heavily against the purchase of the Vincent Black Shadow, and now I tried to dissuade him from buying the gun. When I saw that he wasn't going to listen to my arguments, I stomped out of the store, determined to take the next bus home. I was getting tired of this trip anyway. At the door I realized, once again, I had no money. With what little dignity I could muster, I stomped back across the wooden floor to where Chad was with the gun and demanded, "Are you going to give me money for the bus, or do I have to hitchhike?"

Just then a rancher came up and put his hand on Chad's shoulder. Chad had taken off all of his insignia, and the man did not know he was an officer. "Soldier," he said, "You come out to my place to hunt. We've got lots of antelope on our ranch." It turned out that he would receive a bounty of $5.00 for every antelope shot on his ranch. He was driving a pickup truck around with hunters piled in the back, but they hadn't shot an antelope yet. So, Chad bought the gun and hunting license, and we headed out to the ranch. The rancher's wife and children welcomed us and directed us out to where we could find the antelope. It was miserable for me on the back of the motorcycle when we traveled cross-country. The crash guards kept the big sagebrush bushes from hitting Chad's legs, but they bounded back just right to give my legs a good whop. I was in a bad mood. I was tired and depressed, realizing that Chad had spent most of the money he had earned, and I didn't enjoy this antelope hunt at all. Soon we saw a herd of antelope. I was far-sighted, and Chad was near-sighted in those days, so he hollered to me, "Which one is the biggest?"

"Who cares about the biggest, just shoot one, and let's go home!" was my response.

Soon we tried stalking the animals on foot. This didn't seem too smart either as the antelope can travel about 60 miles per hour. My job was to herd them around a small knoll towards Chad who had the gun. He was just getting ready to shoot a medium-sized antelope when a great, huge buck came thundering around the knoll. Chad shot him through the heart going about 60 miles per hour. Chad was delighted. He gutted him out and then started thinking about how he was going to get the animal back to the ranch. He decided to leave me at a water hole where he could find me again and with my help lifted the heavy animal onto the back of the Triumph, hanging off on both sides. Off he went triumphantly, and I lay down in the sagebrush by the watering hole and went to sleep.

Back at the ranch house, the rancher's wife was looking out the window. She knew that two of us had gone off to hunt. Now she could see the motorcycle returning with just one person on it. Then she saw what to her looked like another person draped over the back. She ran out of the house screaming. She thought Chad had shot me and was bringing back the body.

When the rancher couple saw that Chad had shot a huge antelope, they both were elated. The wife drove out to the watering hole to pick me up, and the rancher got ready to take Chad and the antelope to town. I awoke with the feeling that someone was staring at me. I sat up and found myself surrounded by white-faced cattle, no doubt wondering who this strange creature was at their watering hole. Just then the rancher's wife drove up and took me back to the house. The antelope was tied to the windmill, and there was just time to take a few pictures before the men drove off. When they returned, they were all ecstatic. The rancher had told the story all over town, how he had driven all these big time hunters all over his ranch, and they couldn't hit a thing. Then this young soldier and his wife went out and in no time came back with this huge antelope. When weighed in, our antelope took first place in the contest hands down, however Chad didn't win the prize, as he was not there to register the first day of the contest. Chad had the head mounted and all the meat cut up and packaged and shipped to Minneapolis. That pretty much took care of the rest of the money he had earned in Colorado.

The remainder of the trip home was cold and rainy. How I envied other travelers in their warm, dry cars. The next night we had to turn in to a tourist cabin to warm up and dry out, wasting more of our dwindling resources. Chad actually poured water out of his boots. His tucked in pant legs had funneled the water into his boots. Luckily the cabin had a wood-burning stove, and we dried our socks, boots, and other clothes.

The next day we started out warm and dry but our troubles weren't over. The rear tire blew out going about fifty miles per hour. Chad was able to bring the cycle to a safe stop but was alarmed when he realized what could have happened if it had been the front tire instead. I remember that the last night out we sat up all night in a cafe, drinking strong, black coffee. We had no money for anything else. (Chad was to say later concerning the old saying, "two can live as cheaply as one," that two married people could live about as cheaply as four single people.)

When we arrived at my parents' house, we agreed -- home had never looked so good. And there to greet us was the blue house trailer of my dreams parked alongside our '37 Chrysler in my parents' backyard. Dad and Mother had gone to Chicago and bought the blue trailer with the loan from Miss Twine, pulled it back to Minneapolis, and packed and moved our belongings out of the university G.I. trailer into our own blue dream home.

Chad shot a trophy-sized antelope.

Chapter 16

Playing With Fire

Minneapolis, Texas & Oklahoma
    Sept. 1950

Now we had to get back to reality. The first thing to do was to get ourselves registered for fall quarter at the University. This would be my last year before graduation, and I was eagerly looking forward to doing the student teaching requirement in Minneapolis area classrooms. To my dismay, when I presented the tuition bill to Dad, he refused to pay it. He said he had already paid for my summer session at the university, and since I had canceled out, I could just use my refund to pay my fall tuition. I had kind of suspected this might happen, and I couldn't say a word. He had no obligation to keep paying my tuition, and besides, we were sleeping in our house trailer, but we were putting our feet under his table three times a day. Mother and Dad were always so happy to have us kids around and never charged us a thing for staying there. Nevertheless now we had the problem of paying my tuition. We had used up every cent we had.

However, Chad had an option up his sleeve. During all his time in the army part of his pay each month was in the form of a U.S. Savings Bond. They had been sent to his home address. These had been issued jointly to Chad and Jean Stendal, since she was his beneficiary before he was married. Now he decided the time had come to cash in some of his savings bonds and pay my tuition. To his great surprise, his mother had already cashed in half of them. She felt entitled to half since her name appeared on each one. When he recovered from this shock, he cashed in the others and paid my tuition. He also went ahead and sold the Triumph motorcycle and also the Famous James. (After the tire blowout, he lost interest in motorcycling.) That left us with only the '37 Chrysler for transportation.

I was used to taking the streetcar and bus to the University. The fare was very cheap, 10 cents a ride, or you could buy tokens and bring the price down to 7 1/2 cents a ride. Dad had the lifelong custom of asking me every time I went out the front door if I needed money. Then he would dole me out a dollar. I always hated this, and tried to work and earn my own pin money. I then tried to sneak out the door when he wasn't in the living room. However now I was just happy to take advantage of his generosity. I determined to get through with my education as soon as possible so I could start bringing home a paycheck.

We wanted to be independent, so we investigated trailer parks, and found to our chagrin that it cost $25 a month just for a parking spot. At the University Village, that same monthly amount included water, fuel oil, and electricity. We had no choice but to leave the trailer in my parent's backyard. Then the weather turned cold, and we found that the blue trailer had very little insulation. Even with the oil burner on, it was too cold to live in, so we had to move into my parent's house. They had a finished bedroom in the basement where we could sleep.

I read the College of Education bulletin with a fine-toothed comb and discovered some interesting details. By March I could finish all my required courses, leaving only electives to bring my total credits up to the number required for graduation. Going on into the fine print of the bulletin, I discovered a provision for "quality credits." One credit point towards graduation would be given for every three points earned above a 'C.' Since I had always gotten A's and B's, the way I figured it, I was due 12 quality credit points. That would make me eligible to graduate on March 21, 1951. I took the bulletin to the College of Education office. The counselor looked at that fine print as though she had never seen it before, but it was true. I could finish all my other requirements in the winter quarter and graduate on March 21. In contrast Chad had only completed two years of a five-year course.

One day in December Chad came home very excited. He had been down to the Army Reserve Headquarters and had signed up for an army school of nine months duration. He would be trained as an army aviator and artillery observer. "I'll be able to collect hazardous duty pay and not even have to jump out of the airplane," he rejoiced.

This time I joined him on the Greyhound bus, but after a few exciting days in Waco, Texas, I had to leave Chad in Texas and return forlornly to finish my last quarter at the University. The trip seemed endless as I rode alone through the Midwestern states. Looking out the bus window, everything looked a blue-gray — the sky, the dirty snow — all the same color, punctuated by tan and brown bushes and trees without any leaves. Yet when I got used to it, I could see that there was a certain charm to it all. I knew what I must do and resolved to do my best — to finish my quarter with good grades, organize my house trailer and wedding gifts in preparation to go to Texas after March 21, to exercise regularly, and to sew myself some new clothes for the big occasion of moving to Texas.

As my classes started, I found that my student teaching assignment was in the suburb of Richfield, beyond the scope of the Minneapolis - St. Paul transit system. This meant that I had to drive the old Chrysler every day. This was way before the days of plug in heaters to start cars in cold weather, but Dad had some tricks up his sleeve. We started the car and warmed it up just before bedtime and put a heavy rug on the snow-covered ground under the engine. We also covered the hood with rugs and blankets. The old vehicle almost always started for me.

I must confess that since our marriage, our spiritual life had cooled off. We gradually had allowed the cares and affairs of life to crowd out our relationship with the Lord. There was not an abrupt change, just a gradual cooling off and gradual disinterest in the things of the Spirit. Sometimes the old fears threatened to envelop me again, but I turned them away by telling myself, "I am just as much saved as any other professing Christian that I know." I always did well in the examinations given at the university. I always prayed beforehand, asking God's help and blessing on the examination. I took my good grades as a sign that I must be all right with God, otherwise why would He answer my prayers. One day I heard my mother say that she always prayed for me whenever she knew I was having an exam. I began to wonder if it was her prayers or mine that were being answered.

At the beginning of his pilot training, Chad was in Waco where he made a number of solid, mature Christian friends. His letters were vibrant with comments about his Christian companions and how they were going forward with the Lord together. One pilot in a flight class ahead of him had memorized over a thousand Bible verses, using the Navigator system — the same one I had used after Medicine Lake, only now much more advanced and organized. Chad was trying to follow his example. He could hardly wait until I could join him to share in the spiritual progress that he was making. I could hardly wait either.

Early 1951 turned out to be a record year for snowfall. Dad kept the driveway and the area where I parked the Chrysler well shoveled, but in doing so, the blue house trailer was almost buried. As March arrived, it became evident that the blue house trailer was not going anywhere until after the spring thaw. The heavy snowfall continued unabated. I had to revise my plan.

The day before I was to receive my degree — the Bachelor of Science in Elementary Education — I packed the trunk and back seat of the Chrysler with all the things I would need — linens, dishes, etc. — to set up housekeeping in Texas. My black cap and gown with the maroon and gold tassels and the honor student braid for my shoulder were all ready. We all piled into Dad's car to go to the University. At the last minute, Dad's excitement over his daughter's graduation caused him to flood the engine of his automobile. Expert mechanic that he was, he was so nervous, he couldn't get it started. We finally had to pile into the Chrysler, with Dorothe and me sitting on top of the boxes in the back seat, and arrived at the University barely in the nick of time. I was the last one in the line-up of the graduates, pinning on my honors braid even as we marched down the aisle in the huge Northrop Auditorium. Russell and Jean Stendal were there too, proud as peacocks, and Jean with uncharacteristic kindness whispered in my ear that my walk across the stage to receive my diploma was very graceful.

The next morning I arose bright and early. Dorothe was on Easter vacation, and she planned to accompany me to Texas and return on the bus as I had done in December. To our great disappointment, not only had more snow fallen, but also Minneapolis and southern Minnesota were in the throes of a late spring blizzard. All day Dorothe and I listened to the radio waiting for weather conditions to change, but the snow and wind continued. At 5:00 a.m. the next morning, I heard on the radio that the Greyhound

Dorothe.

buses were running. "If they can get through, we can too," I rejoiced. Dad was not so sure. He stood sadly waving in the driveway as we took off. He later told us that he never expected to see either one of us again.

After several harrowing skids and spins, we finally came out of the snow at Des Moines, Iowa. How wonderful it felt to have firm, black pavement under our wheels, instead of slippery ice and snow. But our troubles were not over. Chad had told me to call him from Des Moines, so I pulled into a filling station and called. The news was not good. "Turn around and go back," Chad told me. He had not done well on one of his test flights. His instructor had washed him out of the course, and all that remained was the elimination ride with a different instructor. No one had ever been reinstated in the course on the basis of the elimination ride. Chad was planning to be home in a few days.

"No way am I going back through that snow and ice," I told him. "Just stay where you are, and we will come down to Texas and pick you up."

When we arrived in San Marcos, Texas, Chad greeted us with a big smile. The unusual had happened. The elimination ride instructor thought he was a great pilot and reinstated him in the course. Dorothe returned to Minneapolis on the bus to finish her last year at Minnehaha Academy. We found an apartment near the airbase, and I took a secretarial job in one of the Air Force offices. I looked forward to meeting the Christian friends that Chad had met in Waco, but most of them had finished their training and gone on to other areas. We were not able to recapture the close fellowship that Chad had known in Waco. Our interest turned to other areas. Chad convinced me that I was mistaken in my stand on movies. He had been an avid movie fan in his youth, and now turned back to this type of diversion. Soon we were going to the movies several times a week. The films were not especially wicked, but certainly wasted time, and did nothing to build up our spiritual lives. We traded the old Chrysler in on a later model Fraser. We now had a car with a radio, and

Chad would browse through the dial on the way to the movies. Every now and then, he would tune in to the Back to the Bible broadcast with Theodore Epp. Dr. Epp's voice was like a voice calling from my past. I didn't like to hear it and was relieved when Chad would turn to a different program.

Our apartment was in a big house on a hill with a large front porch and a swing. Steep steps led down to the street where the cars were parked. The house had been divided to form our apartment, and we had two large rooms, the former living and dining rooms, with a small kitchen and bath behind. We used the former dining room between the living room and kitchen as a bedroom, and I had a beautiful white chenille bedspread, a wedding gift, on the bed.

I didn't have much experience in cooking when I got married, but I had been doing the family baking since Grandma Winburn died when I was fourteen. However, Chad was a meat and potatoes man. He didn't care for fancy food, especially desserts. He would eat an occasional piece of chocolate cake or lemon meringue pie, but I liked to try new recipes. Baking was my hobby; trying new things was like an adventure, but I couldn't get Chad involved. One day I baked banana cupcakes, each one piled high with sticky white frosting. I proudly offered one to Chad when he returned from flying.

Chad stood in the kitchen doorway in his crisply starched khaki uniform and refused to try even one bite of my beautiful cupcakes, the results of my afternoon's labor. All of a sudden something just snapped in my head. It was too much. I was so angry with him. I grabbed one of my sticky cupcakes and hurled it at him. He ducked, and the cupcake sailed through the doorway and landed sticky side down on my lovely bedspread. I grabbed the next one and threw it with more force. The same thing happened. Soon the entire afternoon's baking was upside down on my bedspread. We stood there looking at each other for an instant. Then Chad broke the silence, "Well, if that's the kind of person you are, I'm out of here." (This is more or less what I remember.)

Part Two: A Vision is Formed

He turned on his heel in a sharp, military manner and strode towards the door. In my rage, I grabbed a Jell-O salad I had just made chock full of delicious fruit, marshmallows, and walnuts out of the refrigerator and scooped it into the garbage. Just then I heard a car start up down on the street. I hadn't really thought he would leave.

I threw down the Jell-O mold and tore frantically through the house, across the porch and down the steps screaming, "Honey! Honey! Don't go! Come back!" When I got almost to the street, I realized that our car was parked neatly at the curb, and Chad was nowhere to be seen. It had been a different car that had started up. I turned around and went slowly up the steps. At the top I found Chad sitting in the porch swing having a good laugh at my expense. I was so relieved that he hadn't gone and left me stranded alone in Texas that I forgave him and started to clean up the mess. I don't think Chad ever understood why I got so mad just because he wouldn't try a banana cupcake.

I made friends with one of the pilot's wives who had been in the Christian group in Waco. She had several little daughters, and I invited them over the next Saturday afternoon to help me bake cookies. They had a wonderful time and took the cookies home with them, so Chad didn't have to eat any. I was learning. I had thought that I was being a good wife and homemaker by making a lot of goodies. My dad would have loved that, but Chad would rather have me repel down a mountainside. After this, whenever I baked something, I took at least half of it over to the neighbors.

During this time, we took a Saturday trip to Mexico with a fellow officer of Chad's and his wife. I was appalled at the change that took place at the border. Signs of poverty and filth were everywhere. A young teenager ran past with a sawed-off shotgun. We browsed several tourist shops and bought several items to take back to Minnesota as gifts. We were very happy to cross the bridge to the north side of the river again.

I had had a very sheltered childhood, but deep inside I had a hidden longing for the things of the world, although the only contact I had had with the worldly life style was the comics in the Sunday newspaper. In June, Chad's class was to move to Fort Sill, Oklahoma, to further their training. The officers were throwing a farewell party. Chad planned to ignore the whole thing, but I found out about it and begged to go. Of course I had no idea what I was getting into. At first we sat in a booth with another couple. Chad had told me about this man. He had a wife and three children somewhere in Indiana, but he was running around with a local girl and passing himself off as single. After awhile the girl asked me to accompany her to the ladies' room. There she broke down and started to cry. She said the officer in question had promised to marry her, and now he was leaving for Fort Sill without saying a word about marriage. To complicate the matter, she had just discovered that she was pregnant. I was speechless. I didn't know how to tell her that he had a wife and children somewhere else. As I came out of the ladies' room, distressed to the core, I was grabbed by another officer who was now a little drunk. He wanted to dance with me. I had never known anything about dancing. I tried to get away from him, and another one grabbed me. I looked around for Chad and saw him heading for the door. I wrenched myself away from the officers, who were now starting to crowd around me, and got out the door right behind Chad. "Why didn't you help me?" I demanded. "You were the one who wanted to come here," was his only reply. I realized later that he didn't want to get into a fight with his fellow officers, as that would have magnified the problem. I was a very sober girl as we drove home. If this was what the "world" was like, I wanted no part of it.

In a few days, we packed up our belongings and drove to Fort Sill. Chad now sported pilots' wings on his uniform. Mother and Dad met us there with the blue house trailer that had finally thawed out of the Minnesota ice. We ended up parking in a lot between two shiny aluminum trailers. Behind us was a miniature golf course. The temperature went over 100 F. every day, and our dark blue trailer soaked in the heat like a sponge, as it had very little insulation.

The miniature golf course got very lively at night and continued into the wee hours. They had three records that they played over and over again. I can still hear those three songs in my mind. The only good thing about our location was that beyond the golf course was a watermelon stand that sold delicious, ice-cold watermelon.

The flight training that Chad was taking was very dangerous. He was being trained as an army aviator. These pilots would fly over the enemy lines, reporting back to the artillery and directing their fire. They were unarmed, depending on their maneuverability and acrobatics for their defense . I later learned that their life expectancy in Korea was three weeks. They were also trained to fly at night, landing on unlighted airstrips. The class ahead of Chad had lost a plane, killing both student and instructor. Chad was always telling me of the close calls he or classmates were having. My emotions were on a razor edge. I especially dreaded the two nighttime solo flights he would have to make.

Late one afternoon, Chad came home for supper and announced that he would have to go right back to the airbase for his first nighttime solo. I was so scared and worried. I cried and cried and begged him not to go. Of course, since he was in the U.S. Army, staying home was not an option. At dusk he climbed into the car and took off for the Army base. As soon as he left, I decided that I better do something to cheer myself up, so I went over to the watermelon stand and bought half a watermelon. Upon arrival at the airstrip Chad found that the night flights had been postponed, and when he unexpectedly opened the door of the house trailer, to his surprise, he found his erstwhile grieving wife, happily devouring half a juicy, red watermelon.

Sometimes in the evenings after Chad got home from the flight school, we went over to a new trailer lot to look at a display of beautiful, shiny aluminum trailers with luxurious, designer-planned interiors. The Spartan Aircraft Company had retooled their factory to produce luxury house trailers for peacetime. As we relaxed in air-conditioned comfort on the sofa of the demonstration model, we dreamed of owning one of these beautiful creations someday, instead of the blue "hot box" that we had.

In late August, I bade Chad a tearful goodbye, climbed on the Greyhound bus again and headed for Minneapolis. I had signed a contract to teach fourth grade in a South Minneapolis school. Chad would finish his flight training a month later in time to register for fall quarter at the University.

As I prepared my classroom for the first day of school, I felt mixed emotions. I loved the feeling of being back in a grade school classroom again. The physical plant was similar to the school I had attended less than two miles away. My coworkers were, for the most part, middle-aged, motherly ladies such as had taught me some ten years before. They were very helpful and supportive of me as I started my first year of teaching. However I did not feel grown up nor mature enough to take responsibility for the thirty-nine youngsters who would file into my classroom the next morning. I had celebrated my 21st birthday a few months earlier, but I still felt far from being an adult.

My graduation picture when I got my degree in Education from the U. of Minnesota. The colored braid indicates that I graduated "with distinction." March 1951

136   Minnesota Mom in the Land of the Ancient Mother
Part Two: A Vision is Formed

However as I walked to the school from my parent's house the next morning, passing the familiar yards in which late summer flowers still bloomed, the insecurity was gone. As I started the school day, the friendly affection of the children, and the familiar routine reassured me. I was off to my first happy year as a Minneapolis grade school teacher.

Here I am as a 4th grade teacher at Windom Elementary School in Minneapolis.

Classes were very large back then.

Volume II
A Vision Is Formed

Pat Love Chad

Married, June 10, 1950

Volume II
A Vision Is Formed

Top of the World

Volume II
A Vision Is Formed

Summer

Fall

I
Is Formed

Lake Cabin

Volum
A Visi

Grandpa Dick, Sharon, Russell and Chaddy

Sharon with her doll

As Formed

Chaddy, Daddy and Sharon

Chaddy, Sharon and Russell

Volume II
A Vision Is Formed

Three Generations of Women

*Three Generations of Men,
but Sharon got herself in there anyway*

Chapter 17

Up and Down

Minneapolis, Minnesota
1951

The date came and passed for Chad's arrival. We waited and waited, but he did not come. A telephone call had informed us that he was leaving Oklahoma pulling the trailer, and Dad was worried. He was not at all sure that Chad was competent enough to pull an old trailer with an old car all the way across the country. At last a phone call came from Kansas. There had been some trouble with the gears on a hill, but the car would soon be fixed, and Chad would be home.

A few days later to my surprise, here came Chad with the Fraser, but behind him was not the same old blue house trailer, but the shiny aluminum Spartan trailer of our dreams. Now that I was earning a paycheck, we found a trailer park out in a suburb and set up housekeeping. We had paid off the loan to Miss Twine with Chad's army pay, and now I would have to make the monthly payments on the Spartan. The finances would be tight, but we could just make it. Chad's monthy check of $105.00 from the G.I. bill would help too.

Part Two: A Vision is Formed

The trailer park was newly made on property that had once been an asparagus farm. I soon discovered that asparagus was still growing underneath our housetrailer. If I lacked a vegetable for supper, I could crawl under our trailer and pick some asparagus. Deprived of sunlight, it was white or yellow rather than green. But we thought it was fine.

Fall and winter passed. Chad was back at the University again. We had gotten out of the habit of going to church, and we did not start again when we returned to the Minneapolis area. Our trailer park was far away from Bethesda church. Some weekends we went out to Chad's parents' lake place. They were in the process of restoring a small cabin that was over 100 years old. After a five-day workweek, Jean and Russ spent their weekends working at the cabin. I sensed the friction between Chad and his parents and tried to minimize the differences. They took special offense when Chad made any allusions to Christianity. On occasion, Chad's dad would mock him, calling him "missionary boy." I sensed that being a missionary was about as low as one could get on the Stendals' scale of values. However, there was little chance of Chad becoming a missionary. He also had become a disciple of my dad and had adopted his doctrinal position on just about everything, including foreign missions.

In Texas Chad had started learning verses from the Navigator Memory system, but now with his studies, he soon lost interest. I memorized the verses walking to and from school as long as we still lived with my parents. One really spoke to me. It was I Peter 1:4 *Whereby are given unto us exceeding great and precious promises: that by these ye might be partakers of the divine nature, having escaped the corruption that is in the world through lust.*

As I walked along Lyndale Avenue, meditating on this verse, I thought back to the farewell party at San Marcos. I had been very upset by this experience. Chad told me that the whole thing was status quo for the army. From the pregnant girl whose married lover had broken his promise to marry her, the drinking, the dancing, it was all based on lust. Was that how most of the rest of the world lived? Chad said it was. That was why he never went to the army social functions. I attended several of the citywide parties given for the new teachers. It seemed there were two choices for entertainment — play cards in a smoke-filled room, or engage in square dancing and get pawed by some of the other teachers' husbands. It was all based on lust! It made me sick! Couldn't people just be sociable and talk and have a good time? Here was a verse that promised escape from the corruption that was in the world through lust. The promise was there, but I couldn't quite grasp it. I studied the verses before and after, but I couldn't actually enter into the full significance of the promise, yet I knew it was there. There was an escape from the corruption that was in the world through lust, if I could only find it.

I enjoyed teaching. I had a wonderful group of children, several of whom made it clear that they came from Christian homes. Two Christian mothers asked me to help them start a Child Evangelism class after school, and I obliged. I tried to use different techniques from the pressure tactics that had been so upsetting to me as a child. No one was forced to do anything that made them feel uncomfortable.

Chad's courses were demanding and left him little free time, although we managed to get out to a symphony concert once in awhile. A weekly army reserve drill and ten hours of flying time a month also had to be worked into Chad's busy schedule. I longed for more social activity and kept pestering my husband to go out and mix with other couples, but Chad was too tied to his studies. He had never smoked but had enjoyed beer before his conversion. Now he started bringing a six-pack home to drink over the weekend. He even sent me to the store one Sunday morning to buy him a six-pack. I was chagrined when the storekeeper told me that it was illegal to buy beer on Sunday morning. I would have to wait until 12:00 noon. It was as though a dagger stabbed my heart when I realized that we had sunk lower than even normal worldly people. Even the decent people of the town knew that you should be in church, not out buying beer on Sunday morning.

Part Two: A Vision is Formed

One day, as if waking up and seeing how far from God he was, Chad mumbled something about me being like a weight tied around his neck to hold him down. "I can't live the Christian life married to you," he grumbled. This remark made me feel very sad and reawakened in me the insecurity and doubts of my salvation with which I had always struggled, but which for some years now had been repressed.

One Saturday afternoon, as I washed some baking dishes at the kitchen sink, and Chad relaxed on the sofa, we heard a knock on the door of our trailer. Chad opened the door, and there stood a young couple just a little older than we were. The man had a large black Bible under his arm. They looked a little nervous, but the young man, whose name was John, started telling us the way of salvation and invited us to a neighborhood Bible study that was to be held in a large house across the street.

I told them that we were Christians, but they didn't seem to believe me. I saw John looking at some beer cans that Chad had left on the floor in front of the sofa. I walked over as casually as I could and kicked them under the couch. As we kept insisting that we were Christians, John finally suggested that we pray together for the rest of the people who lived in the trailer court. Chad prayed with them, but I found I couldn't. The old fear had gripped me again, and I went to the bedroom and closed the door.

(As we got to know this couple better, we learned that for weeks God had been laying a heavy burden on their hearts to evangelize by visiting the other trailers in the park. They had started with us as our trailer was the biggest, newest, and most intimidating.)

I did attend the Bible study meetings across the street. I had to go alone as they were held on Thursdays, the evening of Chad's army reserve drill. It was like breath of sweet spring air to be studying the Bible again. However my happiness did not last long. Chad came home from the university and told me that he had signed up to go to Alaska to work during the coming summer vacation. He would work with the Alaska Road

Commission. It was all arranged. He would travel to Seattle by bus, and then be flown at government expense to Alaska.

This news plunged me into the depths of deepest despair. Ever since grade school I had longed to see Alaska. For Chad to go and leave me behind seemed more than I could bear. My mind explored every possibility, but there was no way I could go. We did not have the money to pay for my transportation, and Chad would not give up his exciting summer job. Chad had become my whole life. I had not kept in contact with my former friends. School would be out soon after he left, and I had nothing to look forward to but three months alone. I was trapped. I cried and pleaded but to no avail. I finally got so angry that I wanted to do something utterly horrible to pay Chad back for making me suffer so much. I contemplated the injustices of life. First my father stood in the way of my happiness. Now I had married Chad, expecting to be happy, and he was making me miserable. I decided that life was not worth living. I remembered that some years back a neighbor woman had gassed herself by putting her head in the oven. I began to think about doing the same. I imagined how sad Chad would be to come home and find me dead. He would then understand how miserable he had made me.

Chad was enrolled in an ethics course that quarter, and questions brought up in this class drove him into Bible study. One Friday afternoon, he told me that he had just learned that you couldn't make an intelligent decision unless you knew both sides of the issue. This rang a bell in my heart, and a light went on in my head. There were two worlds out there. One was the Christian world in which I had been raised. I had struggled against the rules and restrictions and wanted more freedom, but I certainly didn't want to go to hell. The other one was the worldly world that seemed so glamorous and attractive, but now that I had tried it out a little, I found it was built on the corruption of lust. I saw that I could now make an intelligent choice between the two. And I knew I wanted to choose the Christian world.

Part Two: A Vision is Formed

The next day was Saturday. Since Chad's parents were visiting their relatives in Norway, and we were supposed to be taking care of their house, we decided to take our week's laundry over there. I would wash our clothes, while Chad mowed the lawn. Their washing machine was an ancient wringer model down in the basement. It plugged into a socket that hung from a cord suspended from the basement ceiling. I filled the machine and plugged it in. The pump to empty the water was on, and water came shooting out all over the basement floor. Then the wringer malfunctioned, and I couldn't turn it off. In desperation, I grabbed the electric socket hanging from the ceiling with one hand while with the other I tried to disconnect the washing machine plug — all this while standing with one foot in the water that had spilled. Electric current ran down both of my arms and out my leg that was in the water. A severe pain centered in my right side, and with all my might I pulled my hands away from the cords. I knew that I had disconnected the machine and let go of the cords only in the nick of time.

Badly shaken, I went over and sat on the basement steps. My arms were both numb, and the sharp pain continued in my side. I knew that I had had a very close call. I remembered my plan to take my own life. I remembered my thought of the day before about being able to make a decision for God. Finally, only one thought was in my mind. "Now that I have reached the place where I can make an intelligent decision for God, the devil has tried to take my life before I actually do it."

I knew that action was needed. The next morning, which was Sunday, Chad and I were seated near the front in Bethesda Church. The sermon seemed tailored to meet my needs and closed with a challenge based on the verse: *He who loves his life shall lose it; he who hates his life in this world shall find it.* John 12:25. Up to this point, I had thought that the main object in life was to be happy, to avoid pain and to seek non-sinful pleasurable experiences. Now I saw that I should give all my life to Christ, even if it meant suffering and unhappiness in this life, and I supposed that it would.

I almost died by electrocution.

I completely surrender my life to God.

Rapelling down a mountain in Alaska.

At last I learned to do it!

Chapter 18

Agony and Victory

As I sat in my pew near the front of the church, contemplating the decision I knew I must make, a thought hit me. I know it came from the devil. "The sermon is coming to an end. If you make this decision, soon there will be an invitation, and you will have to go forward. You have taught Sunday school and Bible school in this church. You got married here, and everyone thinks you are a fine Christian girl. You don't want to make a spectacle of yourself."

I didn't care. I couldn't go on that way any longer. I bowed my head and inwardly committed all of my life to the Lord, come what may. To my surprise, the service closed with a hymn, and no invitation to pass forward was given. As we stood to leave, I realized that the weighty burden on my heart that had bothered me for so long was gone. In its place was the peace and joy of the Lord that I had heard others speak of but had never before been able to enter into for myself. I had an urgent desire to share my experience with others. Since we had not attended the church for a long time, a number of people came over to greet us. I shocked them by saying, using the only vocabulary I knew, "I have just been saved! I was never saved before!" The people were dumfounded. This did not fit their theology at all. "Once saved, always saved" was their motto, and they saw me as having been saved years ago, back when I prayed at my mother's knee. Mother was in the congregation. She came over to invite us home for Sunday dinner. She couldn't believe my story either, but was glad that I had experienced some kind of a breakthrough with God. At home I told the whole story to my dad. Surprisingly he accepted the whole thing. "I always knew you were never saved before," he told me.

Looking back through the years, I do not see salvation as just a point in time, once for all experience, but a continual growth in grace as long as we are in this world. Our faith and commitment to God has to deepen and mature. The decision that I made that morning was definitely a watershed experience in my life. The grace of God had certainly been in my life before but as a little candle shining in a dark place. Now it was as if an electric light bulb had been turned on, and my entire being was illuminated. The best that I can do in summing up this experience is to say that in my previous spiritual experience, I wanted to be right with God in order to escape punishment. The rest of my life was not in focus. Now I had come to the end of my rope, and I was able to make an unconditional surrender as my last hope, like a drowning person grasping a lifeline.

As a part of my new surrender to Christ, I had yielded on Chad's trip to Alaska. I hoped that he would change his mind and stay home, but he didn't. I stood by while he packed his duffel bag for the land of the midnight sun. Nevertheless, when the evening of departure came, and I drove Chad to the bus station for the journey to Seattle where he would catch the plane for Alaska, I was disconsolate. After driving home to the lonely house trailer, I sobbed all night. I longed to talk with someone who would understand how terrible I felt. I thought of jumping in the old Fraser and chasing the bus. The three months that he would be gone seemed to me like an eternity. As I wept through the long night I thought, "Here I am in agony and no one cares or understands. I have no one to turn to." I finally fell into a troubled sleep, and when I awakened in the morning to my consternation, I found my eyes were swollen shut. When I finally got them open by applying ice water, black dots were floating all around on my field of vision. Frantically I applied more ice water and some eye drops, as I had to go to my classroom.

It was the day for our Child Evangelism class after school. We had assigned some memory work to the children, and one little girl wanted to say her verses to me. She had memorized a portion out of Luke 22. As she recited her verses recounting Jesus' struggle in the Garden of Gethsemane, one phrase stood out to me: *And being in agony, he prayed more earnestly . . .* Suddenly, I knew that I was not alone in my grief. Jesus too had been in agony of heart. He knew and understood. He would be there for me. That night I was not alone in the house trailer. Jesus was there with me. For the first time I began to know and depend on Him as a daily friend and companion.

I asked the Lord what to do with the long summer stretching ahead of me. He directed my thoughts towards the Daily Vacation Bible Schools again. I called Northwestern Bible School, and they put me in contact with the Iowa Rural Bible Crusade. The Fraser was getting old and was leaking oil, and Chad had left me with a big red dog that had come to our house as a stray. (I am not a dog-lover, and that dog was a big trial to me, but I had to take care of him for Chad's sake.) That summer was a time of learning to walk with and depend upon the Lord as my companion. All summer I went from rural community to rural community holding Bible classes and closing programs as I had done in Minnesota before. Sometimes a girl from the community helped me with the younger children. Once in a while I had an experienced partner sent by the Bible Crusade. Many weeks I was the only teacher, but Jesus and the big red dog always accompanied me. I tried to communicate to the children and their parents the peace and joy that I had found with a complete commitment and daily walk with the Lord. At the end of the closing program, an invitation was always given for those who wished to open their hearts to the Lord to indicate their desire by raising their hands. I can't remember too much response in Minnesota, but in Iowa many hands were raised. In one community the response was 100%, including the girl who had been assigned as my helper. I never had any more contact with the Iowa Bible Crusade or any of these people, but I trust that I will see many of them in heaven.

The offerings from the closing programs were just enough to cover supplies and buy gas and oil to get to the next community. In the very same week that I came down with typhoid fever, I was fortunate that my partner was a graduate nurse preparing for missionary service in Africa. She felt that my illness was good experience for her in her preparation for the mission field. She said that on the mission field, she would need to evaluate cases in remote areas to decide if she could handle the situation herself or call in a doctor. In my case she called the doctor.

I returned to Minneapolis at the end of August, still a little weak from the typhoid fever, to start another school year. A few weeks later Chad returned with a full beard and lots of Alaskan stories and artifacts. He got off the bus unannounced in downtown Minneapolis on a Sunday morning and found my dad sitting in his Gospel Car on his usual corner. Chad stuck his bearded face in the car window and mumbled, "Can you tell me what the gospel is?" Dad sat for a moment thinking of how to answer this eccentric person when he saw the twinkle in Chad's eyes and recognized him. Dad brought him home in the Gospel Car, and thoroughly enjoyed all the stories of Alaska.

We did not settle back into our old routine. We remembered the little Oxboro church where we had gone as young people and found it to be quite close to our trailer park. Soon we were deeply involved in the work of the church. Chad was a lieutenant in the Boys' Christian Service Brigade, and I became a Pioneer Girls' Guide. These were Christian organizations something like Boy Scouts and Girl Scouts. Our motto in Pioneer Girls was: "Christ in every phase of a girl's life." The first part of every meeting was devoted to games, handicrafts, outdoor activities, etc. After a bridge of singing, starting with fun songs and ending with devotional choruses, a short message was given by one of the guides. There was also an achievement program with a variety of badges to be earned to meet any girl's interests. I really threw myself into this work, knowing what a difference a program like this would have made to me in my troubled years. As requested by these organizations, we each signed a promise to separate ourselves from all worldly practices so as not to be a stumbling block to the young people. We also enrolled in a missions course in the evening school of the Northwestern Bible Institute.

During the year, Chad traded the tired old Fraser for a later model Nash Rambler station wagon. This was a small station wagon with just enough room in the back for a person to lie down. The next summer, in 1953, Chad again signed up to work on the Alaska highways. This time, however, when school was out, I jumped in the Nash Rambler and took off for the Alaska Highway, the Alcan, as it was called in those days. A relative accompanied me as far as Edmonton, Canada, and then I was alone. I would have even welcomed the precence of the dog, but he had been hit and killed by a car in Minneapolis. Once again I had to depend solely on Jesus as my friend and companion as I traveled 2,000 miles through the beautiful mountain wilderness of northern Canada and Alaska. I drove almost nonstop, only sleeping in the back of the station wagon once in awhile. The almost 24 hours of daylight made me want to keep going.

In Edmonton with the Nash Rambler I had to drive 500 miles on a wet, muddy road like this before I got to Mile 0 of the Alaska Highway.

Part Two: A Vision is Formed

I made two little friends in Dawson Creek, British Colombia.

One incident was noteworthy. I purchased a copy of *The Milepost,* a mile by mile travel guide for travelers on the Alaska Highway. It was small and skinny compared to the present day *Milepost,* but it described everything of interest along the 1,500 miles of highway, including service stops for gas, car repairs, and meals. Roadhouses, as they were called were far apart and infrequent in 1953.

By reading *The Milepost,* I was surprised to find that another road, the Haines Highway, branched off from the Alaska Highway about 100 miles beyond Whitehorse. This new road had just been opened and led to the town of Haines, a small city on the coast of southwest Alaska. Whitehorse was the largest city in the Yukon Territory, located roughly midway between Dawson Creek, British Colombia, the official starting place of the Alaska Highway, and Fairbanks, Alaska, the terminal point. (Actually, the Alcan, as it was called then, ended at Delta Junction, joining the Richardson Highway which ran from Valdez to Fairbanks.)

By the time I reached Whitehorse, I was tired of driving and took the business route into the town. Whitehorse is now a large, modern city with every amenity, but in those days, it was kind of a frontier town. Main Street looked like something out of an old western movie. It must have been about 10:00 p.m., and although it was still daylight, all the businesses were closed. After driving through Main Street, the route led up a long, steep hill and back to the Alaska Highway. As I was going up the hill, I noticed a large sign saying something about a highway being closed. I was already past it before the meaning registered in my consciousness. Oh well, I thought, not wanting to turn around on that steep hill and go back, it can't be the Alaska Highway that is closed. It must be the Haines Highway. With my mind relieved, I went merrily on my way.

But it **was** the Alaska Highway. After several more hours of driving, I reached the place where the rain-swollen waters of a small river had washed out a bridge.

Whitehorse, Yukon Territory after a rain. It was not the metropolis in 1953 that it is today.

The expanse that had been spanned by the bridge was not so great, just a little farther than a car length. Previously, someone had lashed logs together and attempted to cross in the southbound lane, however a small truck had proved to be too heavy and had broken through. Now the truck was suspended in the gap, and the owners were no where to be seen.

In the northbound lane, right ahead of me, two men had just completed a similar improvised crossing. I parked my little Nash Rambler behind their car and watched as one man inched their vehicle slowly across, following the hand signals of his friend who stood on the other side. I had gotten out of my car to watch the proceedings. I had no idea what to do. I knew that I was not going to try to drive across on these logs, but I hated to go all the way back to Whitehorse and the men told me that the estimated time to fix the bridge was three days.

"We will drive your car across for you, if you want," they offered, adding that I was not to hold them accountable for any damage that might occur. I promised, and the driver got into my car and inched it along according to the signals from his friend. It was around midnight, but there was still light enough to see and even to take pictures.

Part Two: A Vision is Formed

The washed-out bridge crossing.

I walked across on the logs ahead of my car, and they drove the Rambler over to the side where I was standing. All of a sudden, up the highway zoomed a grey sedan, traveling at a rapid pace. He hit the makeshift bridge at a high speed. The logs trembled, but the lashing held, and the grey sedan disappeared in a puff of dust up the highway. My two new friends and I stood shaking our heads in wonderment and disbelief. It seemed that the driver of the grey car had not even noticed that something was out of the ordinary.

After two or three more days of driving I reached Delta Junction and turned south on the Richardson. Chad was at Trim's Camp, mile 212 on the Richardson--right in the middle of the Alaska range of mountains. As I headed south, the cloud cover lifted, and I was treated to a spectacular view of the high peaks. When I arrived at Trim's Camp, the men had just finished their evening meal. Chad set up our tent. He had told me to bring everything I would need to spend the summer, so I had a tent, sleeping bag and air mattress, a case of beanie wienies and a canned heat stove to warm them up. (I don't think I have ever eaten a can of beanie wienies since.)

There were two other women at Trim's Camp that summer. The resident engineer's wife had four children and lived in a large house trailer. The other woman, Mae, lived with her husband in a very small house trailer. Chad took one look at the case of beanie wienies and decided to continue to eat in the Alaska Road Commission kitchen where they had steak several times a week, home-baked bread, and pie every day. Women were not allowed in the Alaska Road Commission dining room, but Matt Sundberg, the old Swedish cook, took pity on me and let me sit inside the kitchen door on a small bench. I told him about my dad's Swedish heritage, and we became good friends. He appointed me official "pie tester" and also "Kool-aid and iced tea tester." "I just want to make sure this stuff doesn't kill somebody," he would say with mock seriousness as he served me a large piece of pie or a cold drink. Every now and then he would slip a napkin-wrapped steak into Chad's hand and say, "Take this home to the Mrs."

Eventually Mae asked me to share meals with them. I paid 1/3 of the food bill and helped with the work. We had a wonderful time baking bread and making meals in Mae's tiny kitchen. A truck driver came through about every 10 days. We would give him our shopping list, and he would bring us our supplies on his next trip. One time I chased him for fifty miles over the winding mountain gravel road in the Nash Rambler. He had forgotten to leave our eggs.

Again I'm sure I was a disappointment to Chad because of my lack of interest in long weekend hiking trips. I did, however, go on one climb into the mountains, and I did finally learn to repel down the mountainside. More to my liking, I made friends with a Presbyterian pastor and his family that came up the highway. I visited them at their home in Fairbanks for several days and later accompanied them to a Christian summer camp near Anchorage where I volunteered as a counselor to the high school girls for a week.

Back at Trim's Camp, I watched fascinated as the days gradually got shorter. All the leaves and vegetation changed to glorious autumn colors, and a light snow that looked like powdered sugar covered the tops of the mountains surrounding Trim's Campl Every morning the snow-line was a little lower. I wondered how many days it would take to reach our tent.

Chad's contract ended just before Labor Day, and my teaching job started the day after Labor Day. He decided to drive back down the highway with me instead of flying to Seattle, so we had to make the whole trip in just four days. I did arrive one day late even though we tried to drive day and night, one person sleeping in the back while the other took a turn at the wheel. Once a filling station attendant warned me that a pair of men's shoes was sticking out the back of the station wagon. Chad had let the tailgate down so he could stretch out. We had a record number of flat tires on this trip. The last one occurred late at night our last night out. I was sleeping in the back of the station wagon, and Chad was inside a filling station drinking coffee while an attendant repaired our spare. Chad looked up just in time to see the attendant open the back door of the station wagon and throw the repaired spare inside. He had no idea anyone was sleeping there. I was so tired, I didn't even wake up. We arrived in Minneapolis at 3:00 a.m., and at 8:00 I was at school, ready to meet my new class. We had quite a lesson in Alaskan geography that day.

"Morning Watch" at Pioneer girls' Camp Cherith.

Chapter 19

The Promised Land

During the fall of 1953 and on into 1954, I became even more involved in the Pioneer Girl's program. At church I worked with the junior high school girls, called Colonists. Since we had only one boy in our Child Evangelism class that was held in the neighborhood where I was teaching fourth grade, the Christian mothers and I decided to change the program to Pioneer Girls. The grade school division was called Pilgrims. This drew in quite a few new girls from the other grade-school classrooms. Together with some of the women from our church, I started to attend periodic guides meetings for the whole Twin City area. There we learned new techniques and ideas for our weekly meetings and enjoyed fellowship with like-minded women from all over Minneapolis, St. Paul, and the suburbs. Soon I was asked to join the camp committee that planned and ran the annual summer camp. To my great surprise, at the first meeting, I was appointed chairman.

The deep spiritual fellowship that I enjoyed with my fellow Pioneer Girls workers filled a void in my life. Yet I was still a strong believer in the ultra-dispensational doctrine, so I felt a bit disloyal to have fellowship with those who were of a different persuasion. Pioneer Girls, as a para-church, international organization functioned in churches of all Bible-believing denominations. My dad was not happy with my participation in Pioneer Girls. I tried to honestly talk to him about it, but he was not interested. "If it has a name, it is not right," was his strongly held opinion.

As winter turned into spring, I was asked to head up the high school division, called Explorers, during the three weeks of summer camp in August. I would be the only counselor for this age-group. This was considered to be the most difficult age to work with, and the whole committee was in agreement that I was the person for this job. We also had a Counsellor in Training program (CIT) that I would be involved in. I accepted this big responsibility with fear and trembling.

As I prepared my Bible studies for the weeks of camp, I was relieved that it was the epistle of Paul to the Colossians that I would be teaching. At that stage of my life, I would have felt uncomfortable teaching James or I John because of my father's strong opinions. As I studied Colossians in depth, using commentaries and other translations, as well as the Pioneer Girls' outline, I was struck by one fact: According to the best authorities that I found in my dad's carefully selected library, and the clear statement of the Bible, the mystery of God was *"Christ in You."* The motto of the Pioneer Girls organization was "Christ in every phase of a girl's life." I felt relieved and confirmed that I had made the right choice in entering so heartily into the ministry of Pioneer Girls in spite of my dad's lack of approval. We leaders of the Pioneer Girls were right in tune with the teachings of the Apostle Paul.

I became so involved in my activities with the Pioneer Girls that in the spring of 1954, when Chad signed up to return to Alaska with the Alaska Road Commission (this time for six, not three months), I waved him off for Alaska without the sense of desolation I had felt two years before. My life had now become very full and complete. Time did not hang heavy on my hands. In addition to my teaching career, I now had the huge responsibility I had undertaken with the Pioneer

Girls as well as my involvement with our local church. Every night of the week except Friday was programmed. I hardly had time to clean the small trailer and wash my clothes.

I finally relaxed from my struggle to reconcile my Dad's teachings with the more general fundamentalist stance of my church and Pioneer Girls. Instead of a feeling of separatism and struggle, engendered by my parents and the ultra-dispensationalists, I thrived in the more comfortable environment of my new friends. We were from diverse parts of the church but united in seeking to reach girls for the Lord and promote our motto of "Christ in every phase of a girl's life." We did not argue about doctrines, but privately we in the inner circle of leadership confessed to one another that we depended heavily on the doctrine of eternal security. We felt that once we achieved our goal of getting a girl to pray the sinner's prayer at camp or in one of our weekly meetings, she was eternally saved from hell and was assured of a place in heaven. One friend confided that without this assurance she would not find the motivation and energy to continue in this emotionally demanding work.

Nevertheless, all of us as leaders were saddened by the fact that we saw so much "backsliding" as we called it. Back in the 1950's there was not much teenage drinking, premarital sex or pregnancies, and no drugs to deal with. The "backsliding" consisted of worldliness, disobedience to parents, lack of interest in church or spiritual activities, and things of that nature. In order to counter this decline we kept the girls going forward spiritually by interesting, fun-filled meetings, and area activities such as winter retreats, sleigh rides, sleepovers at the churches, and area rallies. Each meeting or other activity started with an entertaining activity of games, crafts or sports. This fun-time ended with the singing of rousing folk-songs, rounds, or action songs, starting with the more boisterous, and finally bridging over into lively Christian choruses, and ending with a worship chorus or hymn. Now the stage was set for a Bible-based talk given by one of us coun-

Part Two: A Vision is Formed

selors, one of the same women who had led them in the games, fun or crafts at the beginning of the lesson. Sometimes it was an inspirational story the girls could apply to their own lives. Many times we arranged to have this devotional part of the meeting outside around a campfire. Sometimes the meetings ended with treats, such as roasted marshmallows or smores (graham crackers lined with chocolate squares which then sandwiched a roasted marshmallow).

We also strongly encouraged each girl to have a personal devotional time with the Lord each morning, Morning Watch it was called. An extensive award program centered around personal interests and coordinated with applicable Bible verses and spiritual applications was also stressed. The girls who were the most dedicated to the program acquired uniforms on which to pin their ranks and sew the badges they had earned. We guides were also encouraged to work our way through the award program, and in spite of my heavy schedule, I soon had a number of ranks and badges to display on my sky-blue uniform.

I usually ate Sunday dinner with my parents, but I only shared my experiences in Pioneer Girls with my mother. She had always been an avid soul winner and was happy to see me active in the work of the Lord. Dad and I once again entered a period of "silent truce." I conversed with him on non-controversial subjects, but I felt his strong disapproval of my activities with the Pioneer Girls.

One weekend, on my way back to Minneapolis from a visit to Chad's parents out at their lake cabin, my little Nash Rambler gave up the ghost. A call to dad from a nearby farmhouse brought him to my rescue. He towed my car to his backyard, and an examination showed the engine to be completely worn out. He found the engine full of dirt and silt from the Alaska Highway, and the under carriage so banged by rocks that the gas tank held one gallon less than it had before the Alaska trip. After much grumbling and shaking of his head, he and his good friend, Gunnar, rebuilt the engine.

During the summer I was invited to attend meetings in Chicago where I met the national leadership of the Pioneer Girls organization. The national director confided to one of my friends that had I not been married, she would have invited me to move to Chicago, join the staff and work full time in the organization. As it was, she appointed me Fort Captain, the volunteer leader, for the Minneapolis – St. Paul area. I had my life all together now. I felt fulfilled and happy. In my estimation, I knew the New Testament backwards and forwards, as the saying goes, and could elaborate on any subject or verse as the occasion demanded.

I remember once reading a chapter for our morning devotions to a rather rebellious teenager who was temporarily staying with me in my house trailer. After the reading, I turned to her and remarked, "Is there anything you don't understand in that chapter? (My implication was that if there were, I would explain it to her.) Her reply was in the negative, but the next morning, **she** picked up the Bible and read a chapter to me "Is there anything **you** don't understand in that chapter?" she asked me. I was taken by surprise at her attitude. It was the first hint I had that I might be coming across to some people as a self-righteous prig. Today one might have said I was made of Teflon. I always had an answer for everything. In my own estimation, I knew it all.

In general, the girls seemed to love me, especially the more difficult teenagers who sometimes had issues with some of the other adults. Many times girls confided to me the problems they were having with their parents and siblings at home. I tried to give them good Bible-based advice. I hope it was wise counsel. Some of them cheered my heart by telling me how lucky any children would be, if I ever had any, to have me for a mother. I did want to raise any children I might have in the wisdom and nurture of the Lord, so that they would not have to go through the spiritual and psychological struggles that I had endured.

The summer of 1954 passed quickly. The three-week summer camp in August was a great success. As September loomed on the horizon, I was saddened by the approaching start of the new school year. I loved the life I had lived that summer. I would like to have continued as a full-time Pioneer Girls' worker (although I had not yet been told of the national director's desire to have me on her staff). However, September would also bring Chad's return from Alaska. He still had several years of study left to complete his five-year program in civil engineering at the university. I would have to continue working as the family breadwinner for a few more years.

Vernell Newgard was one of my CIT's (counselors in training) at camp. Our paths would cross again many years later under different circumstances.

Sometime in the late 1954's or early 1955's, another thing happened that broke through my self-satisfied veneer. I attended a Youth for Christ meeting in downtown Minneapolis where Theodore Epp, the head of the Back to the Bible Broadcast, was the advertised speaker. This radio program was a household word in our family, as my mother tuned in frequently to this world-renowned preacher. It was Pastor Epp's voice that had come over our car radio when Chad and I were dabbling in worldliness in Texas, and it was like the voice of God breaking into the wilderness in which we were wandering. In spite of my busy schedule, I made an effort to go to this meeting and hear this great man of God. Chad opted to stay home with his studies, so I had to go alone.

For some reason the preliminaries were very long that evening, and not much time was left for the main speaker. Finally Pastor Epp came out on the stage and said that instead of his planned message, he just wanted to leave a few thoughts with us. His thoughts were from the Old Testament. Of course I was well-versed in all the Old Testament Bible stories and knew something of typology; however I didn't realize that Old Testament happenings had a spiritual application to us today. As well as I can remember, this is what he said:

"Just as the children of Israel came out of Egypt, wandered in the wilderness, and then went into the Promised Land, you can tell where you are in your Christian life by who your enemy is. Egypt is a type of the world. If your struggle is with worldliness, you are still in Egypt. The wilderness is a type of your self-will and the control of the flesh. If your struggles are with sins of the flesh and wanting your own way, your enemy is your self, and you are in the wilderness. The Promised Land is a type of the victorious Christian life. In the Promised Land, you still have battles, but your enemy is Satan, himself. If your struggles are with the spiritual forces of darkness and taking souls away from Satan, you are in the Promised Land."

That is all there was to the message by the famous preacher, but it spoke to my heart. I praised God that I was not now struggling with worldliness. Chad and I had each signed a pledge to keep ourselves apart from all that was considered worldly (smoking, alcoholic beverages, movies, etc.) in order to be accepted as Christian workers with the youth, he with the Christian Service Brigade, and I with the Pioneer Girls organization. However, I could not say that I knew anything about struggles with Satan or the forces of evil. I saw myself in the wilderness, struggling against the sins of self: pride, complacency, and wanting my own way. An idea penetrated my consciousness; perhaps I had not arrived yet spiritually, perhaps there was a higher level to attain. If so, I wanted it. Driving home to the little house trailer in the suburbs, I told God that I wanted to go on with Him. If I was in the wilderness, I wanted to go on into the Promised Land.

In March a new development occured that was life-changing for both Chad and me. After almost five years of marriage, I was pregnant for the first time. The timing was a little inconvenient as Chad still had two years to go at the university. I would not be allowed to continue teaching after the school year ended in June. Chad got a job in construction during summer vacation. (No more talk of Alaska.) I was excited. I felt that motherhood would be the biggest adventure of my life, more exciting even than a trip to Alaska.

In June 1955, I resigned from the Minneapolis Public School system with four years of experience behind me. In August I was still able to go to camp as the Explorer counselor in spite of my pregnancy. Mother even volunteered as one of the camp cooks for a week. I was happy to meet Vurnell Newgard again. She had grown up from the toddler I knew at Elim Chapel. She now was one of our CIT's (Counsellors In Training). I believe I resigned the chairmanship of the camp committee, but kept most of my other duties.

In September we parked our lovely Spartan house trailer on the farm of a friendly family who knew my parents, and Chad and I moved back into 4440 Bryant Ave. Our income would be very skimpy until Chad graduated from the university in June, 1956. He doubled up on classes taking a record 28 credits instead of the usual 18. I acted as his secretary. I made a large chart to keep track of all of his assignments. I learned to use a slide-rule (no calculators in those days) and helped him with his homework. This emergency of an unexpected pregnancy was just the motivation he needed to put forth heroic efforts in his engineering courses.

On the 25th of November, 1955, the first little Stendal baby made his appearance. We named him Russell after his paternal grandfather and Martin after his father (Chadwick Martin). Chad and I both took parenthood very seriously and did everything possible for his well-being, physically, mentally, and spiritually. Chad continued his all-out effort and completed two years of study in one. I took a teaching job in a Minneapolis suburb for one more semester, leaving baby Russell in my mother's care. When Russell was six months old, Chad received his degree in civil engineering and started work for the St. Paul District Corps of Engineers. The next May in 1957, our second son, Chad Lionel, was born.

Russell Martin arrived Nov. 25, 1955 changing our lives forever.

Chad Lionel followed on May 28, 1957.

172 Minnesota Mom in the Land of the Ancient Mother
Part Two: A Vision is Formed

Chapter 20

My Sheep Hear My Voice

Grand Rapids, Minnesota
1957

"Mommy and Russell are soooo lonely," I sighed. With 21-month-old Russell on my lap, I rocked back and forth in the green platform rocker. Baby Chaddy was sleeping in the crib, and Big Chad was out working at the radar station. Grand Rapids in the heart of Minnesota's Land of the Sky Blue Waters was our temporary home. But even the fresh sparkling summer day in this beautiful vacationland did not lift my depression.

I had been used to a heavy schedule of activity in Minneapolis. Now I felt cooped up in this tiny house with two babies to care for. Here there were no Pioneer Girls, no friends, and no helpful mother ready to baby-sit at a moment's notice. Chad's job, the supervision of the construction of three small radar stations, their sites forming a triangle each about a hundred miles from the other in this sportsmens' paradise, required long hours of overtime and frequent trips away from home. I was incredibly bored and lonely.

Part Two: A Vision is Formed

In an attempt to lift my depression, Chad had hired a competent Christian woman to care for the children and sent me to Pioneer Girls' Camp to counsel for a week. I had enjoyed being back at camp again, but I found it hard to relate to the week's theme, which was praise. Now I was back home again, and the depression was returning. I had been asked to write up the requirements for several new badges for the high-school-aged girls. I was knowledgeable about the subjects, but I was physically and mentally unable to write. I felt bound by iron bands. It seemed that I could never get both babies to sleep at the same time, and I had no time for myself or the pursuit of intellectual activities.

Russell in Farmington at 2 1/2 years old.

Over the past two years, Chad and I had pretty much decided that the ultra-dispensational doctrine that we had been taught was in error. The Sunday after my return from camp both of us had submitted to the rite of water baptism, anathema to the ultra-dispensational camp. About this time we accepted and started to apply the entire New Testament as relevant for us today. While at camp I had overheard two of the high school girls in my cabin discussing the relevancy of the Sermon on the Mount (Matthew 5). One believed that it was applicable for us today, while the other was convinced it was for the Jews at a future date, It was the old argument that I knew so well. Realizing that I, an adult counselor, was present, they appealed to me for an opinion. I surprised myself by reversing twenty-seven years of teaching and proclaiming it to be relevant for us today.

Chagrined, the dispensational girl turned to me and demanded my red slacks, quoting with a gleam in her eye, "Give to him who asks." (Matt. 5:42) I instantly realized my predicament. These were my best slacks, the only ones that fit me well. I had bought them new for camp. I had never been asked to do such an outrageous thing in my life, but I saw that if I refused, I had relegated the Sermon on the Mount to history or prophecy. I immediately got the pants and handed them to her.

"I don't want your slacks," she declared with embarrassment. "I was just trying to make a point."

The ringing of the telephone interrupted my mournful reverie. Who could be calling? I knew no one in town. A friendly voice greeted me. I did not know her, she said, but my parents knew her in-laws. My mother had called and asked her friend to help me get acquainted in this town. We started attending our new friends' church and often met after the service in one of our homes for refreshments and fellowship. The church was quite similar to the ones we had been attending. The doctrine was just a bit different, and they were a whole lot stricter about their beliefs. We soon heard by the church grapevine that there was a problem in the church because some people were saying that God spoke to people today. The church believed, as did my dad and most of the people we had fellowship with in Minneapolis, that even though God spoke to individuals in the Bible, we were in a different dispensation now called "The Silence of God." Now that we had the Bible, the doctrine went, God spoke to us only through the printed page.

I wondered about this. My mother, whose personal walk with Christ I respected very much, sometimes spoke of having a "premonition," a knowledge of what was right or wrong or what course of action to take. Was that God speaking to her? I thought back to hymns we sang frequently at home and at church:

"I come to the garden alone,
while the dew is still on the roses,
and the voice I hear, falling on my ear,

> *the Son of God discloses.*
> *And He walks with me and He talks with me,*
> *and He tells me I am His own. . .*

Another was:

> *I walk with the King, halleluia.*
> *I walk with the King, praise His name.*
> *No longer I roam, my soul faces home.*
> *I walk and I talk with the King.*

It seemed that the hymn writers talked to the Lord and experienced the Lord talking to them. The real clincher was a song that was often sung as a special number at Bethesda church. Pastor Prince was very strict in not allowing doctrinally incorrect songs to be sung in the church. Yet a favorite among the singers of duets was:

> *My God and I go in the fields together,*
> *we walk and talk as good friends should and do.*
> *We join our hands, our voices ring with laughter,*
> *My God and I walk in the meadows dew.*

I had never heard any objection to any of these songs. Did it mean that the person was out in the garden or the fields with the Bible, and a verse lit up? Somehow I was sure it was more personal than that.

I also remembered the verse in John 10:27 *My sheep hear my voice, and I know them, and they follow me. . . and the voice of a stranger, they will not follow.* St. John was the one gospel that both my dad and our church accepted and quoted frequently. Even though not written by the Apostle Paul, it seemed to be considered applicable to our day and age.

My dad certainly never mentioned God speaking to him. He studied the Bible, read respected Christian authors of his doctrinal persuasion, and with his sharp intellect figured things out. I pondered this question for several weeks.

One of the men in the group that were now our new friends mentioned Jesus walking and talking with him in the routine of his daily life. His conversations were filled with comments such as: "I said to the Lord . . . The Lord said to me . . ." God was far from silent in this man's life.

"Hey! Wait a minute!" I stopped our friend in mid-paragraph as we sat around in a living room one Sunday evening. "Just how do you get this relationship with the Lord?" Inwardly, I was thinking that if the Lord were that real to me, I wouldn't be so depressed.

Even though I had made a personal contact with Jesus and knew Him in a personal way back in 1952 when Chad went to Alaska the first time, I was something like the Shulamite girl in the Song of Solomon. I had found "my Beloved" and leaned heavily on Him when my need was great — the summer teaching DVBS and the trip up the Alaska Highway alone. But then when I became so active in church and Pioneer Girls' work, surrounded by Christian friends and activities, I lost my focus on the presence of Christ in my life — strangely enough, the very thing we were trying to teach to the Pioneer Girls. Now when the outward trappings were taken away, I found the freshness of His presence was gone. I was left desolate. But God was faithful and sent another group of Christians to seek us out, as He had done before in sending John and Virginia Sponsler to our trailer house.

The reply was ready. "Oh, that's easy! The only thing that stands between you and God is "self'!" That was quite a new thought to me. I can't say I had ever heard a sermon preached on the subject, but I sort of knew what it meant. Self had to do with being selfish, putting your own interests before those of others. After we got home that night, I dropped to my knees by the green platform rocker and asked God to take away the self-centeredness that was insulating me from His fellowship. The next morning, I woke up with songs of praise thundering through my head. All the hymns we had sung at camp suddenly took on new meaning. As I went outside the entire world looked fresh and bright. The grass was greener than I had remembered; the sky was bluer. I was glad to be alive. The depression was gone.

Part Two: A Vision is Formed

Back in Minneapolis, we had been somewhat annoyed by a small group of people in Oxboro church who had insisted on praising the Lord all the time. Some were young people, former members of our youth groups, and others were adult members of the church. They seemed to be on some sort of spiritual inside track that excluded other members, such as Chad and me. I avoided them as much as possible, but Chad would meet them head-on. "Brother Chad, are you praising the Lord today?" a young man would ask after the morning service.

"No, am I supposed to be?" Chad would counter.

Immediately the young fellow would open his oversized Bible and show Chad a verse that said we were to be always praising the Lord. Now, with this new dimension of praise vibrant in my life, I suddenly felt a kinship with those folks back at Oxboro. I could hardly wait to get back to tell them that now I knew what it meant to praise the Lord too.

By this time Chad had accumulated quite a bit of sporting and camping equipment. With our mobile lifestyle, this was becoming a problem. We were thinking of buying a lot by a lake near Grand Rapids and building someplace to store all of our equipment.

A few days after I had prayed for "self" to be removed, Chad too met the Lord in a new and deeper way (his story is told in *High Adventure in Colombia*.) The selfishness that he had developed as an only child, was instantly gone. All of a sudden, Chad, who had always been somewhat antisocial and self-centered, was inviting people home for dinner, He especially tended to invite missionaries who came to speak at the little church we were attending, and often offered them the pick of his treasured possessions — guns, cameras, and sporting goods. By the time we returned to Minneapolis for the coldest winter months (when construction work was closed down in northern Minnesota) we were quite established in our new, unselfish way of life.

Chapter 21

The Vision Grows

Minneapolis and Mexico
1958

Back in Minneapolis, we rented a house from a family who was going to Arizona for the winter. We were happy to be back at Oxboro again but were perplexed at not finding a number of our friends. Chad asked one of the leaders where these people were. He told Chad that they had been asked to leave the church because they were "speaking in tongues." That really astounded us. We really didn't know anything about this subject, so Chad brought it up on Sunday at the Carlson dinner table.

Dad reacted very negatively and said that this was something that had gone out with the Apostles. By this time Dad had narrowed down the Scripture even farther and was only interested in the letters that Paul had written at the end of his life from prison. Chad decided to ask the Lord directly to show him the truth on this matter. One night while praying alone after everyone else had gone to bed, he felt his mouth began to move. As he added voice, strange sounds started coming out. Excitedly, he came to the bedroom, shook me awake, and told me that he had "spoken in tongues." This was the closest I had ever come to the supernatural and I felt a great relief and joy to know that God was willing and able to invade our prosaic world with a supernatural act. However in the morning, I remembered nothing of this incident. Chad probed a bit, asking me if I remembered something he had told me in the night, but since I didn't, he took it as a sign that he wasn't supposed to tell anyone.

Meanwhile, the family that owned the house in which we were living returned unexpectedly from Arizona and wanted to get back into their home. We held a lease for two more months, but we felt very sorry for the children who were staying with a nearby relative and came every afternoon to look mournfully through the windows into their home. Chad had accumulated some vacation time, but who vacations in Minnesota in February?

There was only one solution — go south. Mother offered to keep baby Chaddy, and two-year-old Russell went with us. "We will go south until half of our money is gone, then we will start back," announced Chad. We got all the way to Mexico City before turning around.

"Be careful not to eat any raw vegetables or drink unboiled water," cautioned a friendly doctor in Texas just before we crossed the border into Mexico. Clutching my AAA TourBook, I quickly rolled up the car windows as we pulled into a Mexican filling station. I didn't want any dirty, snotty-nosed youngsters touching Russell's fuzzy blond head. At first we stopped only at hotels and restaurants approved by the AAA where I felt secure. Then Chad, feeling adventurous, took a turn off the beaten track, and we found ourselves in a town with no AAA accommodations. He picked the best-looking motel and got us a room. The next morning when we woke up, it was obvious that this motel would in no way pass inspection by the AAA. I vowed to eat nothing until we got back on the Pan-American Highway and found someplace mentioned in my TourBook.

The Vision Grows 181

By noon I felt sick, weak, and nauseated. "Oh for a hamburger and chocolate malt," I moaned, lying on a hard bed and staring at the stark white fly-specked walls. The fact that I was in the first weeks of pregnancy probably didn't help either. Oh, how I wished I were back north of the border. Would I live to see the good old U.S.A. again? I wondered. I was so afraid that Russell would catch some horrible tropical disease. I felt like I had one already. Chad had taken Russell and gone out sightseeing after I had refused to get up.

"Here, take a look at this!" beamed Chad, coming in off the street. "I was lucky enough to find some real ham from the United States! Look! Here is some bread all sealed in waxed paper and some butter. Look here! It says it is pasteurized, and I got some milk in a carton, just like back home, also pasteurized." The ham sandwich he gave me was delicious, and the milk was just like back in Minneapolis. After eating, I felt better and suggested we go for a ride. We went down to the ocean and looked at some ships, then after touring around the city, we drew near to our hotel. "Look! There is the place I bought the food for lunch," commented Chad as we drove by an open market. In the doorway hung a fly-covered beef carcass, slowly turning green in the hot afternoon sun.

"Oh, no! Not in there!" was my horrified reaction. However, I felt better and we continued south – all the way to Mexico City before we came to the midpoint of our resources.

A week later as we drove north through the desert country of northern Mexico, I marveled at the slim, neatly dressed girls I saw along the road. "How can they look so immaculate coming out of mud huts, washing their clothes in the river, and drying them on the ground?" I wondered aloud. Their pastel cotton dresses were nicely ironed and fit them perfectly. I felt rumpled and dowdy in my waistless shift dress. Peeping into the doorways, I was aghast at the primitiveness of the inside furnishings. "If people live in such scarcity right here by the main highway, what must living conditions be like back in the interior villages," I commented to Chad as we drove along.

Then I remembered Katherine Voitlander. She was a missionary the Pioneer Girls supported financially. Many times I had read her newsletters aloud to the girls. I knew she worked with the Wycliffe Bible Translators in an Indian tribe somewhere out there in the area through which we were passing. I knew that she had to ride many hours on horseback to get to the village where she lived and worked. How I would love to meet her, I thought. I would ask her all my questions about life in those far away villages.

As we continued north, I daydreamed about forming a mission to send luxuries to missionaries like Katherine. Let others worry about the necessities. I would send cake mixes, dehydrated foods, nice-smelling bath powder, colorful blouses of no-iron materials, frilly lingerie, and toys for the Indian children.

Back in Minneapolis, our awakened interest in missions was fed by a series of articles in the Minneapolis newspaper, which would later be known as the Minneapolis Star-Tribune. A few years before, five missionaries had been killed by a savage tribe in Ecuador. Now one of the widows, Elisabeth Elliot, had written a book, and excerpts were being carried by the paper. We marveled at the dedication of these men and the courage of their wives to carry on alone. We searched for information and eagerly devoured the books that became available concerning this venture to reach the Auca tribe. We felt as though these couples were giants in their spiritual maturity, and we were grasshoppers in spite of our many years of intensive Bible study and pride in our doctrinal correctness. We joined the Moody Press book club and were soon introduced to missionary authors such as Isabel Kuhn, Jonathan and Rosalind Goforth, and Adoniram Judson, as well as Hudson Taylor and Amy Carmichael. Over the supper table we shared anecdotes from our current reading.

The Vision Grows   183

Chaddy in Farmington at 1 1/2 years old.

After a brief time back in Grand Rapids, Chad was transferred to Farmington, Minnesota, to be the project engineer for a Nike Missile Base. The sleepy little town was just close enough to the Twin Cities to enable us to resume attendance at Oxboro Free Church and keep in close touch with family and friends. However we still missed the little group at Oxboro who had always been praising the Lord. Chad was able to keep up with his activities with the U.S. Army Reserve and advanced to the rank of captain. He was also able to maintain his flying proficiency with ten hours in the air each month.

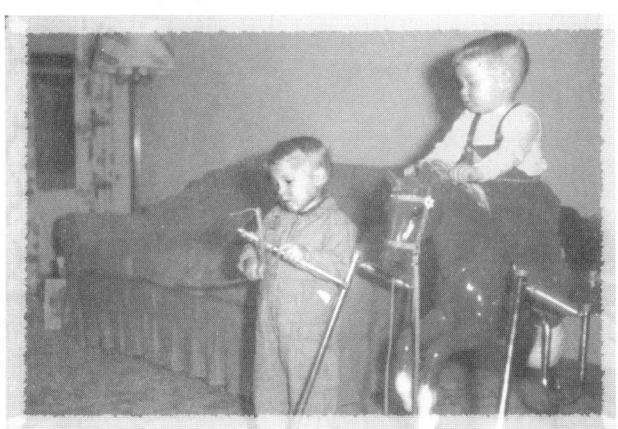
Russell in his railroad engineer's uniform, a gift from Grandpa Russell. Chaddy rides on the rocking horse.

Part Two: A Vision is Formed

John Wesley, circuit riding preacher.

In addition to resuming his involvement in the Christian Service Brigade, Chad's new interest in missions led to his appointment as chairman of the mission board of the church. He also embarked on a personal study of the "Old Time Religion," a theme that led him to the biographies and works of men such as John Wesley, George Whitfield, David Brainerd, and Charles Finney. We had already studied books by A.J. Tozer, A.B. Simpson, Norman Grubb, Rees Howells, and Leonard Ravenhill. I read every minute that I could. I even propped an open book behind the water faucets while I washed the dishes. Russell's favorite toy was a rocking horse. He played at being John Wesley, riding his horse from one town to the next. When he arrived at the make-believe town, he pulled a New Testament out of his pocket, opened it, and recited from memory John 3:16. Then he rode on to the next town. These heroes of the faith were becoming as real to us as the people next door, or our friends from church.

Chapter 22

Katherine's Visit

Farmington, Minnesota
1958

The impending arrival of Sharon Rose in October plus the care of two active little boys curtailed my activities somewhat, but I was able to continue my reading. The lives of these missionary women impressed me greatly. We even found a book by one of Chad's shirt-tail relatives, Marie Monsen, a Norwegian missionary to China*. She was captured by pirates, but her firm faith and indomitable calm in the face of these ruthless men was awe inspiring. She refused their stolen food and lived on a large box of chocolates that the Lord directed her to buy just before boarding the ship. After reading this book, I found one written by one of Marie Monsen's fellow missionaries. I don't remember her name or the title of her book. This woman had the ministry of dealing in depth with each of the missionaries about their past lives, leading them to repent of and forsake anything in thought or deed that might even possibly be construed as sin and thus hinder the flow of the Spirit in their ministries. She

---

*See Appendix.

went from mission station to mission station, and the missionaries from varied missions waited in turn to have a session with her. At the end of the book, she included a checklist taken from Scripture verses. The sins these missionaries repented of were mostly in thought or word, little attitudes of unkindness toward fellow workers, Chinese or foreign, etc. One evening after the children were in bed, I went through the list, repenting of and forsaking all that the Lord showed me. These were mostly things from my childhood and youth, dealing with fantasies, etc. I knew that Marie Monsen had been influenced by this gifted woman. In the months after her ministry to the missionaries in China, revival broke out in that country. This was just before the Communist take-over when savage persecution broke out against missionaries and Chinese Christians.

At the births of each of our sons, I felt that Chad had been very remiss about bringing gifts to the hospital. My roommates had received boxes of chocolates and beautiful flowers from their husbands. As I anticipated another trip to the hospital, I carefully oriented Chad as to his responsibilities. Sharon made her appearance the night that her daddy was out of town on an overnight flight, however in the morning, Chad appeared at the hospital still in his army uniform, his arms loaded with gifts. He didn't bring anything so ordinary as flowers and chocolates however. A huge foam rubber pillow and some new books from the Christian bookstore were Chad's choices.

One of the books, *Words Wanted* by Eunice Pike, told of two young women living in an Indian village in northern Mexico searching for words in which to convey the gospel of St. John into the Indian language. Looking for words — words wanted — the idea intrigued me. I would have liked to have done something like that, I thought. Oh, well, it was too late now. Too bad I hadn't heard about this work before I got married and had all these kids, I thought.

We brought Sharon home from the hospital just three weeks before Russell's third birthday. He was an active, precocious child and was elated with his baby sister. One day a stranger referred to him as a baby. "I'm no baby!" he indignantly stated, drawing himself up to his full stature, "I'm the oldest of three children!" At seventeen months, Chaddy was a cuddly roly-poly. His reddish blond ringlets and big blue eyes reminded folks of the picture on the Gerber's baby food boxes. He was happy and outgoing except when bothered by frequent attacks of allergic bronchitis. His life was changed but little by the new addition to the family.

However I found life much more difficult with three children than with two. Chad tried to be helpful. He sold some of his hunting guns and bought me a much needed clothes dryer. I was still having to get up at night with Chaddy, and now with a new baby waking me up to be fed in the wee hours, I was not getting enough sleep. I trembled on the edge of nervous exhaustion. Since I couldn't train Chaddy to sleep through the night, our doctor suggested that Chad pick one of the two babies and get up with that one while I attended the other. He picked Sharon and soon had her sleeping through the night. Sharon became a "daddy's girl" at a very young age.

In spite of the increased demands on our time, we managed to continue reading about the lives of great Christians. One evening after the children were sleeping, we sat across from each other at the kitchen table and dedicated each of our children to be missionaries, drawing God's attention to each one and asking Him to call each one into His service.

Not long after that, one Sunday evening in the spring of 1959, Chad stayed home with the children so that I could attend the evening service at Oxboro. To my great surprise, the speaker was Katherine Voitlander. Katherine was a soft-spoken young woman in her late twenties who gave an impressive plea for volunteers for Bible translation work in the Amazon basin. Going up to her after the service, I told her of our trip to Mexico and my desire to know more about living conditions in the Indian villages of Mexico. "Wednesday is a free day in my schedule, and I would be glad to spend it with you," was her reply.

I found Katherine to be an easygoing woman of few words. She was a part of a three-woman team assigned to one of the tribes of northern Mexico. Her responses to my many questions were matter of fact. Yes, they ate the beef bought in the market place. No, the flies didn't hurt it; the germs were killed by cooking. Yes, they cut off the green places. No, her living conditions were not too difficult. She would prefer living more like the Indians, but the health of one of her partners would not permit it. No, she did not feel that she was being deprived of the luxuries of modern life. Yes, she did have a special prayer request. Because of her talent in drawing, the director of her mission was requesting that she spend a great deal of time in Mexico City illustrating beginning reading books for other tribes. She would prefer being out in her own tribal location; nevertheless, I was to pray that the Lord's will be done.

I finally got around to sharing with Katherine my feeling that I could have done this kind of work had I known about it years before. "Oh, the children are no problem," she insisted. "You take them right along with you. Lots of families do it." I wasn't so sure.

Chad came home at noon for lunch, and we continued talking on into the afternoon. Before Katherine left, Chad was convinced that the Lord was calling us to attend the linguistic training classes offered by the Summer Institute of Linguistics (SIL) at the University of North Dakota. When I told Katherine that I didn't think I would have much time to accomplish anything with the Indians since the care of the three children took up all my time, she replied in her calm, matter-of-fact way, "After all, being a missionary isn't so much what you do. It is just living among the people and showing them the Christian way of life. You can do that better with a family than as a single person."

After Katherine was gone, I remembered something else she had told me. It was a very new and startling thought. "Sometimes," she said, "I think that God's purpose in sending out missionaries isn't so much the good that it does the people, as the good it does the missionary."

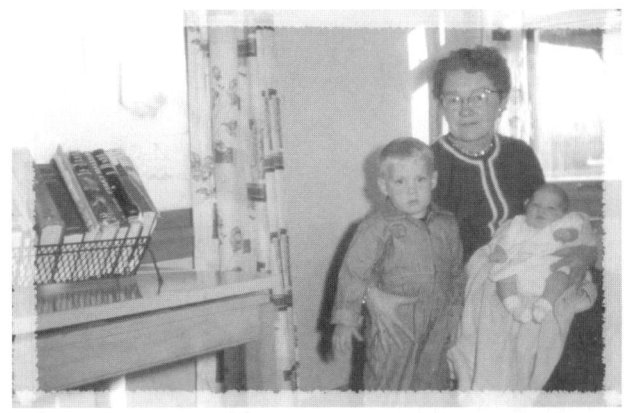

Grandma Jean with Russell and Baby Sharon - Christmas 1958.

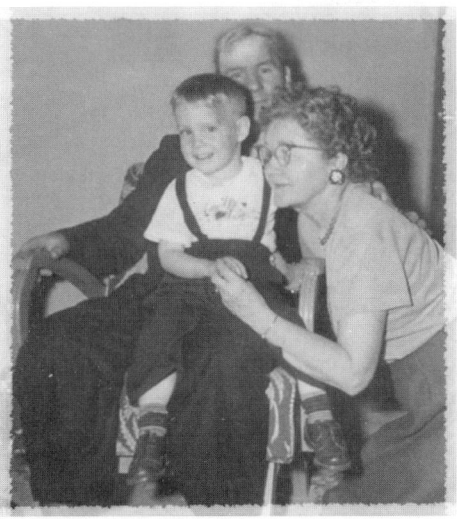

Russell with his Grandparents.

Part Two: A Vision is Formed

Chapter 23

A Delay and Russell's Prayer

After Katherine's visit, Chad sent for application forms and started to make plans to attend the Summer Institute of Linguistics. I was disheartened. I was finding it harder and harder to get through the week. The housekeeping chores piled up. This was before the day of such conveniences as disposable diapers and plastic liners for baby bottles. Most cooking and baking were done "from scratch." Looking back now, I realize that I spent much time baking elaborate goodies that I had to share with the neighbors, as Chad still did not care for desserts. I devoted much time to reading the inspiring Christian biographies that I mentioned before. I also spent much time playing with the children. Russell could recognize all the letters of the alphabet when he was still two. The children were never put to bed without an extensive time of singing, Bible stories, and prayer.

We didn't have a television and rarely turned on the radio. We were still very active in our church, although I had cut back my activities somewhat because of the children. In our house, the children came first, then the Lord's work, then cooking, housekeeping, etc.

Part Two: A Vision is Formed

We had recently purchased a new vacuum cleaner and an automatic washer and dryer with money from the sale of some of Chad's sporting goods. I was enjoying these modern conveniences immensely. I had little desire to give them up and go live in the jungle.

Another problem was the linguistics. I had been out of college for eight years now. How could I go back to studying again? I remembered how poorly I had done in Spanish and Swedish classes in high school, and how I had managed to avoid foreign languages at the University.

As I pondered all this, I realized that I was beginning to have a hard time hearing and understanding Chad. I told him to quit mumbling, and he said I was hard of hearing. I finally went to an ear specialist who confirmed that I suffered from a significant hearing loss in the bass register. As Chad persisted in his plans to go to North Dakota for linguistic training, my hearing became worse and worse.

Finally the morning came when I was so dizzy and nauseated that I couldn't get up out of bed. In desperation Chad called my mother for help. "You've got to get back on your feet again," insisted Mother after several days of chasing the active boys and caring for baby Sharon. "I'm making you an appointment at the Nicollet Clinic for tomorrow morning."

The next day there were no parking spots available near the building where the clinic was located, so Mother and the children circled the block while I went in to see the doctor. He was a friendly young man whom I remembered having seen at our church some weeks before. He and his family were just about ready to leave for Hong Kong as medical missionaries. "Is there anything on your mind that could be bothering you?" he asked me kindly as I finished reciting my symptoms. I poured out the story of the three small children, and Chad's desire to go to North Dakota to study linguistics in preparation for the mission field.

"Well, well," the doctor shook his head sympathetically, "Your body feels it is being asked to do something beyond its capabilities, so it's just making you feel sick so you won't be able to do it. If it were a financial problem, you would have to trust the Lord to supply the money, and if He didn't send it, you couldn't go. If I were you I would just commit this problem to the Lord, and He will either have to change your husband's mind or give you the physical resources that you feel you lack."

At that moment an emergency case arrived, and the doctor had to leave. He turned in the doorway and told me I could wait for a complete physical examination if I wished, but that he thought his analysis of my problem was correct. As I stood outside on the sidewalk, waiting for my mother's car to come past, I committed the situation to the Lord. I did not feel sick again and gradually my hearing improved as well.

About this time the Farmington project was completed, and Chad was chosen to head the initial work on a huge lock and dam to be built on the Mississippi River in downtown Minneapolis, right near the big post office where Dad was still the superintendent of the building. We temporarily moved into 4440 Bryant again. One day Chad came home from work and

Our children and their playmates in front of the Carlson family home, 4440 Bryant Avenue South in Minneapolis.

announced that he really couldn't leave to go to the linguistic summer school until this project was over. I breathed a sigh of relief, and life settled down to normal again. No one, not even my parents knew of the close escape I had had with the mission field.

Both Chad and I felt increasingly uncomfortable with the materialism of the 1950's. The veterans of World War II were home. Most of them, it seemed, had taken advantage of the G.I. bill and earned a college degree. The American economy was booming. Now the veterans were busy buying homes in the suburbs and producing the "baby boomers."

Russell, Sharon, and Chaddy in 1960.

Teachers were in great demand. The grade schools in the suburbs were overflowing with children. Many classrooms were made to serve double duty. The morning shift started at 7:00 a.m. and dismissed at noon. At 1:00 p.m. the afternoon students with a different teacher started, and their school day ended at 5:00.p.m. After Russell was born, I took a job teaching an afternoon class, leaving my mother to care for the baby, but after Chad graduated and got a job with the Corps of Engineers, we decided that I would be a stay-at-home mom.

We tried to downsize instead of going with the materialistic American trend. We kept our living expenses as low as possible in order to have funds to invest in our various youth programs and to send to missionaries in whom we were interested, in adddition to our regular tithe to the church.

The next spring under the Lord's direction, we bought a house in Bloomington, a suburb of Minneapolis not far from Oxboro church. The lovely yard included fruit trees and a garden space. In the upstairs of the house was a knotty pine paneled bedroom for the boys. It was the house of our dreams, and the Lord led in every step of the purchase. Two of our neighbor families were members of our church, and between them had several teenaged daughters who liked to baby-sit, thus freeing Chad and me for church activities. Soon, in addition to the Boys' Brigade, Pioneer Girls and the Mission board, we took responsibility for a teenage Sunday School class, became the adult sponsors for the Senior Young People, and together with another couple conducted a children's church during the regular morning service.

Our own children, especially Russell, were taken along whenever possible. On Sunday afternoons Chad often took our boys and members of the young people's group to visit local nursing homes to sing and testify. On one occassion Russell, aged four, stepped forward and gave a testimony. As soon as his brother finished, Chaddy, aged three, took a step forward and said, "Me too!"

Chad and I were delighted to see signs of spiritual growth in our children. Because of my spiritual struggles as a child, I had at one point decided not to allow my children to make a commitment to the Lord until they were teenagers, so that the step would be more meaningful to them. However this was all taken out of my hands when a week before his second birthday, Russell got down on his knees by the sofa and prayed in a loud voice, "Come into my heart, God! Come into my heart, Jesus!" Then getting to his feet, he thumped his chest with his hand and with a serious look declared to me, "He's in there!"

From that time on he took his place as a Christian, praying freely, testifying, and insisting on long periods of Bible reading from the Berkeley Version of the Old Testament. Sometimes after reading four or five chapters of the adventures of Samuel, David, or other Old Testament heroes, I would just have to get up and get some housework done before the two younger ones woke up from their naps. Occasionally I would have to spank Russell to get him to quit pestering me for more Bible reading. I thought I must be the only mother in world to spank her son because he wouldn't quit demanding more Bible reading.

Chad and I tried to be good parents. We greeted the children in the morning with a hug and a prayer. A short, interesting devotional time was planned each evening according to their ages. At night they went to bed with a Bible story, a kiss, and a prayer. Chad was a strict disciplinarian but was also reasonable and loving. He took his roll as a father very seriously.

One evening when Russell was almost five years old, Chad decided to give him an orientation on missions. He had a large book of pictures depicting the life of a mountain tribe of Indians in Ecuador. As he got into the book, Chad realized that the total effect was grimmer then he had anticipated. The last picture showed a man lying by the side of the road in a drunken stupor after a weekend in town. The wife sat dejectedly beside her husband, protecting him from thieves until he would sober up enough to continue their journey to their mountain village.

Russell was horrified by this way of life and asked his father why they lived like that.

"They don't know the Lord, Son," answered Chad.

"Why don't they know the Lord?" Russell wanted to know.

"Well, I guess because no one has gone to tell them," was the reply.

"Why hasn't anyone gone?" Russell persisted.

By this time Chad was feeling quite uncomfortable and was wishing he had never brought this subject up in the first place. "Well, Son, I guess no one really cares much about them," he replied.

"But you care, don't you, Dad?" Russell's big blue eyes looked up questioningly at his father. Surely anyone as wise and kind as he would do something about these poor Indians.

"Russell, you don't understand," Chad patiently explained. "You can't just up and go to a place like that. God would have to call you. He would have to open the door to the country, provide the money that you would need. Maybe when you are a big boy. . ."

But then Chad realized that Russell wasn't sitting on his lap anymore. He was kneeling beside the sofa praying in a loud voice. "Dear Lord," he prayed, "Please call my parents to be missionaries, so that I don't have to wait until I'm a big boy."

Oh, no, I thought as I listened from the kitchen. I had felt such a relief since Chad had backed off from this idea of being a missionary. Now the subject had come up again, and somehow I felt that Russell's childlike prayer had gone right through the ceiling and straight to Heaven.

Russell about the age when he prayed that God would call his parents to be missionaries.

198   Minnesota Mom in the Land of the Ancient Mother
    Part Two: A Vision is Formed

Two brothers in a tub.

Sharon too has a "swimming pool."

Chapter 24

Vacation Bible School

Bloomington, Minnesota
Summer 1961

The summer rolled around. I had been asked to direct the Vacation Bible School at Oxboro Free Church. In trying to staff the school, I ran into problems. It seemed that no one wanted to take any responsibility. After lining up a provisional staff, I realized that I had promised to help almost every departmental supervisor. I didn't know where to start, and who to help first.

Although I had resigned the chairmanship of the Pioneer Girls' Camp Committee, I was still the camp registrar. Since the camp was in August, I had thought that it would not interfere with the VBS in June, but I had forgotten that we had moved the registration deadline forward. To my chagrin, the mail started bringing camp registrations the week before the VBS was due to start. Everything was hitting at once.

Wednesday evening at prayer meeting, an Oxboro mother handed me a camp registration form and a check, which I placed in my purse. The next evening at a VBS planning session, she mentioned her daughter's camp registration.

Part Two: A Vision is Formed

Our new home had a lovely back yard with fruit trees, a garden plot, and raspberry bushes.

"But your daughter hasn't registered yet," I replied.

"Yes, she has. I gave it to you last night," she insisted, "You put it in your purse. Look and see!"

I opened my purse, and there was the registration and the check. The ladies laughed, but I was startled. I had no memory of the transaction. Was my mind starting to fail? I felt like a generator with too many appliances plugged into it. A fuse was about to blow.

After driving home from the meeting, I dropped down on my knees by the sofa. "Oh, Lord!" I cried, "I've really done it now. I shouldn't have accepted so many responsibilities. I've promised to help too many people, and I don't know where to start. Please help me!"

The next afternoon, I decided to tackle the huge basket of ironing that had accumulated. This was before the days of perma-press or easy care fabrics, and I was always behind in the ironing. The children and I would need lots of clean clothes to carry us through the two weeks of Bible School that would start on Monday.

It was a beautiful, sunny afternoon in early June, but there was still a slight chill in the Minnesota air. Russell came to ask if he could blow up the wading pool. "A wonderful idea," I thought, "That will keep them happy all afternoon, and I can finish this ironing." But as we were filling the pool with the garden hose, I realized that the water was too cold. I couldn't have them sick now on top of everything else. Suddenly I had an idea! I would carry out a pail of hot water from the basement to add to the cold water from the hose. Running the hot water faucet full blast in the laundry tub, I quickly filled a large plastic bucket full of steaming water. "One big pail of this good, hot water will do it,""I told Russell.

Half way to the wading pool, the bucket broke. The extreme heat had melted one side where the handle was attached. Steaming hot water poured onto my foot. I quickly pulled off my tennis shoe and ankle sock just in time to see layer after layer of skin burst and shrivel up. After an initial intense pain, I felt nothing.

A neighbor drove me to the doctor. "You have a third degree burn," he told me, "which will most likely require a skin graft. However," the doctor continued," we are experimenting with a new treatment for burns. We will dress your foot, then you are to go home, stay in bed with your foot elevated, and keep as still as possible. If new skin starts to form, and your foot swells, the new skin will be destroyed, and you will have to have the skin graft. Return in one week, and do not remove the dressing."

By this time it was late Friday afternoon, and the VBS was to start on Monday. I called each one of the department superintendents, and after hearing of my accident, each one promised to handle her department without further help. It seemed that everyone who heard the news came to the rescue. The three children all went off to Bible School on the church bus each morning. Mother came to accompany me in the daytime, and the neighbors took turns bringing in delicious suppers every evening. At the end of the first week, the doctor was delighted with my progress. Proudly he showed me the little gray lines, which were the new skin. Once again he applied the special dressing and ordered another week of bed rest with the foot elevated and repeated the warning that under no circumstances was I to walk on that foot. (We had rented a pair of crutches for absolutely necessary mobility.)

At the end of the second week, the doctor removed the bandage, and lo and behold, the foot was fine — no scar and no skin graft. Two days later I was able to attend the closing program of the VBS and present the certificates and awards. I could not help but note the wonderful enthusiasm and unity among the staff. Everyone agreed. It had been the best Vacation Bible School the church had had in years.

Majel Meyer.

Chapter 25

Majel Meyer

During my two weeks of enforced bed rest, I was able to process all the camp registrations. I also found time to read a book that had been attracting my attention for weeks. It was entitled *Where Are the Thousand?* and was directed to those who had been attracted to missions by the deaths of the five martyred missionaries in Ecuador but who had never gone to the mission field. The author, Majel Meyer, had been a short-term missionary in Peru in the 50's. Seeing the need among the Indian tribes of the Amazon Basin, she had been impressed to pray for a thousand new missionaries for the Indians of South America. The Auca massacre with its resultant publicity for missions had been the answer, she felt, to awaken American young people to the great need in South America. Several important and widely read books had been written by Elisabeth Elliot, the wife of Jim Elliot, and Rachel Saint, the sister of Nate Saint, two of the martyrs. Yet, few of those people whose attention had been captured by the incident had actually presented themselves for missionary service. "Why?" Mrs. Meyer asked herself.

In her book, *Where Are the Thousand?*, she suggested that perhaps it was because the people called by the tragedy had been too attached to physical comforts and conveniences and lacked the spiritual power and victory in their lives to overcome these carnal desires. I could identify in what she was saying. The point hit home. I remembered my misery in Tampico, Mexico, and how I had longed for a U.S. style hamburger and malted milk. I had enjoyed short camping experiences in a primitive setting but always within the familiar safety of the United States or Canada. I had to confess to having an terrifying horror of tropical diseases and parasites, especially for my children, but for myself as well. I also dreaded the inconvenience of being faced with a foreign language. I had no illusions about my language learning ability. I had always enjoyed being considered clever in any type of learning situation, and from my short stay in Mexico, I already realized how moving into an area where one is unfamiliar with the language reduces one to the status of a stammering, babbling child again. The author of this book explained and illustrated by personal experience how she had found victory over these problems through the old-time Methodist doctrine of sanctification.

As I read through the book, I felt that I was probably one of the thousand of whom she spoke. Chad and I had been very impacted by the news of the death of the five missionaries in Ecuador. After our return from Mexico, we had read all the books that had been written about the incident. The biography of Jim Elliot had been especially meaningful and challenging to Chad as he was born the same year as Jim Elliot. We were undoubtedly two of the thousand this woman had been praying for, but we had not volunteered for missionary service for the same reasons that she stated in her book.

I wondered about this doctrine of sanctification. It was never mentioned in any of the churches we had attended. I knew that my dad was dead set against the teaching. Chad had become very impressed with the writings of the early Methodists. He frequented the used bookstores of downtown Minneapolis, bringing home piles of books, mostly covered with moldy leather and filled with tiny archaic writing.

He poured over these books night after night after the children and I had gone to bed.

I asked Mother for her opinion, as I knew she had been a member of a Wesleyan Methodist congregation before she was married, but her present estimation of the Methodists was not too favorable. According to her judgment, they all went forward once a year at the revival meeting to "get saved" once again and never seemed to progress much beyond that point.

Since our experiences in Grand Rapids, Chad had been involved in an intensive Bible study of his own. He was seeking an answer to the question that continually plagued him: Why had his own Christian life gone so well right after his conversion when he was in the army with just the Bible and the Lord's presence, and why had it gone downhill once he got out of the army and into the fellowship of a local church.

He also sought to know why the church that he saw then in the 1950's and early 1960's was so weak and powerless in comparison with the church in the time of the Wesleys and the Great Awakenings in the United States. Now in 2009, we look back with nostalgia to the churches we knew in the 50's and 60's.

The first "church-learned doctrine" that Chad had thrown out of his belief system was that of "eternal security." This was a fundamental doctrine of all of the churches we had attended, and was also firmly believed by my parents. In fact, we were quite prepared to argue as long as necessary to convince people of the truth of this doctrine. However, Chad now felt that in these Christian circles in which we moved, this idea had been overstated and was serving to lull people into a complacent stagnation. Strangely enough, this was also the starting point for Majel Meyer's argument. As I held a certain reserve towards Chad's discoveries, I also felt a restraint towards Mrs. Meyer's teachings. In view of the years of struggle I had undergone to feel some measure of security, I just did not feel able to open up that question to the possibility of doubt again. Yet as I read on in the book, much of what Mrs. Meyer said was quite convincing. Her challenge of overcoming the world and the flesh was compelling. I found myself wondering what kind of a person she really was. Is she some kind of a "religious kook," I thought, or is she a reasonable stable person in normal life? If I could only meet her, I thought, I could tell if her argument should be taken seriously.

Towards the end of my second week in bed, I received a phone call from an old friend from church whom I hadn't seen in years. She invited me to a weekly prayer meeting and mentioned that the next Tuesday they were having as a guest speaker a woman who had been in Peru and who had written a book. I immediately realized that this was the author of the book I was reading. Here was my chance to meet Majel Meyer face to face and decide if she was believable.

And so it was that the next Tuesday morning, I walked into Ruth Haase's living room and encountered a group of ladies who were sitting around in sort of a circle singing choruses. Over half of these women had been among the group who was always praising the Lord at Oxboro years before. Although I had always prided myself in being able to keep my emotions in check, as I sat there among these old time friends, many of whom I had respected greatly for their Christian vitality and close walk with the Lord, I was astounded to find myself on the verge of tears. The music seemed to penetrate to my very soul.

After awhile Ruth started to speak. "Pat," she said, after welcoming me to the group, "Everyone who comes here has agreed to answer honestly three questions. Are you willing?"

"Go right ahead," I replied, although not without some misgivings. In some strange way I had always considered myself superior to these women, although certainly not in spiritual stature. Perhaps it was because I had been a professional woman when they were motherly housewives. I had first seen Ruth at Oxboro with her little brood of children when Chad and I had come in the group of young people from Bethesda to present the monthly program. Now, here I was, the mother with young children, and these women were welcoming their first grandchildren.

"First," continued Ruth, "Do you know that you are saved?"

I inwardly rejoiced that in spite of my many years of doubt and torment, I could answer this question in the affirmative.

"Next, do you have a pure heart?"

This question took me by surprise. I had never been quizzed on this point before, although after reading *Where Are the Thousand?*, I had some idea what was meant by a pure heart. The problem was that over the weekend I had had a severe argument with Chad for which I felt at least half at fault. With that kind of behavior in my recent past, I just could not declare that I had a pure heart. The ladies patiently opened their Bibles to verses that clearly stated the necessity of a pure heart. Did I want to have one, they asked me. Why yes, I did!

Meanwhile, I kept looking around at the few unfamiliar women in the circle, trying to figure out which one might be the missionary from Peru. One lady explained to me that having a pure heart was having confessed all your sins one by one and having placed each one on the cross of Calvary. I knew that I had never done that. We all got down on our knees by our chairs, and I was asked to confess the first sin that came to mind, repenting of it, and placing it on the cross, then take the next item, etc. until there were no more. It was just like emptying out a large basket of dirty clothes, one by one.

At one point I hesitated. It seemed just too humiliating to get down on my knees like that in front of these women. Hadn't I been in the same church with most of them for years? Hadn't I played a leading part and been considered as "spiritual" as anyone else? One woman must have noticed my hesitation. She assured me that they were sworn to not gossip about anything that might be said in the meeting. I got down on my knees, and truly it was like entering the narrow gate, or the camel going through the eye of the needle. (It is interesting to note that the sins that the Lord brought to my mind at this time were current, attitudes and anger at Chad and the children. The past sins that I had repented of when I read about the missionaries in China did not come to mind again. They were gone.) At last only one item remained. I felt that it was between my mother and myself and that I must talk with her directly about it. The ladies graciously accepted this statement and did not pry or press me to tell them. By now the time was gone, several had already gathered their belongings and left. The meeting was dismissed.

It was only after I arrived home that I realized that I had not met Majel Meyer. I later learned that she had been suddenly called to her home in South Dakota and had not attended the meeting. In my disappointment, I could not have imagined the big role she would play later on in all of our lives.

Chapter 26

Old Cars and a Risky Trip

The next Tuesday morning found me back in Ruth Haase's living room again. I had just experienced the most joyous week of my life. It seemed as if a huge burden had been lifted from my shoulders. Although not one of the sins I had visualized being placed on the cross the previous Tuesday were of much consequence, the overall effect of feeling that my heart was pure and clean before God and man was exhilarating. I had explained and apologized to my mother and had written two letters admitting wrong-doing and asking forgiveness. Now I was back in the circle of ladies waiting to hear what Ruth's third question would be.

Ruth explained that the class had been set up on the lines of the old-time Methodist class meetings where each member gave the state of his soul. The last question was probably the most important and was asked of all members: Are you walking in victory?

From then on, I hardly missed a Tuesday morning meeting. Sometimes we gathered again at Ruth's home on Tuesday nights for a watch night service, also a Methodist custom. On these occasions we prayed for the burdens of one another's hearts and also around the world for international problems and situations. Some of these petitions have had amazing answers in later years.

(For those who don't understand, a watch night service is a time when people come together at bedtime, instead of going to bed, and pray all night or until all the burdens on the hearts of the participants have been prayed through before the Lord. This was a kind of fasting, going without sleep instead of going without food. The next day, one was expected to get up at the usual time and go about normal activities, not sleep late or take a nap.)

My goal was to walk into Ruth's living room one Tuesday morning and announce that I was "walking in victory." However it seemed that every Tuesday morning as the ladies were singing, the Spirit of God would speak to my heart about some additional area of my life that needed attention. One by one my phobias were dealt with; one day it was my relationship with my mother-in-law; another morning it was my reluctance to go out to dinner at an exclusive country club restaurant when invited by some of Chad's relatives. (The Lord even provided just the right dress for the occasion.) All these and much more came to the foreground on Tuesday mornings. It is true that in some of these areas much more work was needed in future years, but in each case basic groundwork was laid and correct attitudes and motives were formed. The ladies were patient and understanding as they prayed me through my problems. Several of them became virtual big sisters to me.

As summer turned into fall, Russell started first grade. After much prayer, we decided to send him to a Christian school in downtown Minneapolis. Although we were out in the suburbs, beyond the end of the bus route, a Christian family from the school was willing to keep Russell in the morning until time for the bus. He could ride into the city with Chad in the morning, and then in the afternoon return to the friend's house on the bus and stay until Chad picked him up after work. It was a sacrifice for me to have Russell away from home for such a long time each day. However after meeting his first grade teacher and the mother of the family where he would stay before and after school, I knew that we had made the right decision. They were both women who would build into his life "gold, silver, and precious stones." (I Cor. 3:12)

At the end of September, Chad sprang another bombshell. He was going to Montana for two months to work on a special missile project. Before I could believe it, he was gone.

All of a sudden, I was confronted with handling all the problems of suburban living alone. The worst problem was that of getting Russell to the place where he would catch his bus each morning. Chaddy and Sharon had to be awakened out of a deep sleep, stuffed into snowsuits and carried to a cold automobile. I didn't

Russell returns from his first day at school.

dare to leave them at home alone sleeping for the forty minutes or so that I would be gone. Both of our cars were old, hard to start, and not yet tuned up for cold weather. The mornings were getting increasingly brisk, and on several occasions I found frost on the ground when I emerged from the cozy warmth of the house into the nippy chill of the autumn dawn with my sleepy crew.

My best chance of success in starting a vehicle was on the first attempt. If that failed, the only hope for that car was to let it sit until the rays of the rising sun warmed it a bit. Instead of waiting, I would then pass with all three children to the second car and with increasing nervous tension try again. If

Part Two: A Vision is Formed

I could hear well enough to give the engine gas right at the critical second, all would be well. If not, Russell would be forced to miss a day of school, or else I would have to drive him all the way to downtown Minneapolis in the early morning rush hour traffic after things had warmed up, and one of the cars had decided to start. Invariably either Chaddy or Sharon would be irritable and miserable and would start to fuss, Russell would start giving me unwanted advice, or a fight would break out among the three just at the crucial moment when I needed to concentrate on the sounds coming from the engine. Subjected to these pressures and irritations, my temper would explode, and I would scream threats and warnings at the children through clenched teeth and strike them with blows that they could hardly feel through their heavy snowsuits. Of course I had learned this kind of parental behavior at home from my Daddy Dick, but it was conduct that I detested and in which I had resolved to never engage. Afterwards, whether the cars started or not, I would feel emotionally drained and guilty.

One Tuesday morning this all came out at the prayer meeting. After counsel and prayer, I grasped the fact that I could rest in the Lord even in this matter of getting Russell to school. I would commit the whole thing to the Lord before we left the house. Whether or not the cars started, I would keep my serenity. What a victory! After that, the first car tended to start on the first try too.

Just as I was feeling confident in my new role of single parent, another bomb exploded. A letter from Chad suggested that I might like to drive out and visit him in Montana, bringing all three children along. He was getting lonely and would like to see us all. Before the arrival of the children, I too loved adventure, spur-of-the-moment trips made against the advice of older, wiser heads. However, now that I had the responsibility for three little lives besides my own, I found that I also had a strong sensible and practical tendency. I certainly did not intend to hazard the lives of my children on such a foolhardy venture. The cars were both old and unreliable, and at this date a blizzard in the Dakotas or Montana was not at all unlikely. Besides, Russell would miss at least a week of first grade.

My parents agreed with me that this was a foolish idea, and I felt good about my decision to stay at home. That is, I felt good until the next Tuesday at prayer meeting. Once again, during the singing, I felt deeply troubled. Later in the meeting, I shared the problem with the ladies. While agreeing that my decision was based on good sense, they felt that God might have some reason for wanting us to go. They advised me to get in touch with Chad, and if he really was serious about the trip, to launch out on faith.

That evening Chad called and confirmed that he really did want us to come. In his estimation, the old Mercury, the better of our two cars, was reliable enough to make the trip, even if it was hard to start on cold mornings. Russell's teacher considered the trip a wonderful educational opportunity, and my mother offered to accompany me and visit the relatives in South Dakota en route. We had a delightful trip, praying about every overnight stop and overtly trusting the Lord for everything. The dreaded blizzard occurred, but not until Chad was with us to do the driving as we visited relatives from his side of the family on the weekend in Montana.

On Sunday afternoon, Chad drove us out of the snowy area toward the Dakota border. Monday, in the wee hours of the early morning, I drove him to the bus to go back to his job in central Montana. Sharon had especially enjoyed seeing her Daddy again. A few weeks before the trip, she had turned to me and asked, "Why don't you go out and get a job so that my Daddy can stay home and take care of me?"

This Monday morning, October 23, 1961, was Sharon's third birthday, and although Chad would not be able to share it with her, he had several carefully chosen presents giftwrapped and ready. Birthdays had been very important in Chad's family. "Be sure that Sharon has a nice birthday,"

Part Two: A Vision is Formed

Chad said as he prepared to board the bus. "Just because you are traveling, don't neglect to have a party. Stop at noon and buy a birthday cake, and then give her the presents."

Back at the hotel, as soon as Sharon opened her eyes, she realized that it was her birthday. At once she started talking about the wonderful day she was going to have, including a huge birthday cake with lots of colors — white, pink, purple, green, and brown. Land sakes alive, I thought. How am I ever going to produce a cake like that in the middle of Montana or South Dakota? Together with Mother, we committed our day to the Lord and started off.

Noon found us in a small town right near the border. I drove down the main street, looking for a bakery. There it was, the only one in town. In the window was a very small, round chocolate cake. That will never do, I thought, not for Sharon's birthday. She wouldn't even consider that a birthday cake. I went up to a girl behind the counter, "Do you have anything that I could possibly use for a little girl's birthday cake?" I asked her hopefully.

"What's her name?" the sales girl abruptly questioned, and hardly waiting for my reply, she rushed into the back room. In a few minutes she returned with a huge cake in her hands. The white frosting was intricately decorated with all the colors that Sharon had mentioned — pink, purple, green — and right in the middle, large brown letters proclaimed, "Happy Birthday Sharon!"

"I'm sorry I appeared rude," apologized the sales girl. "I knew that two birthday cakes had been ordered. The first one already said 'Happy Birthday Betty.' I rushed out hoping to stop the decorator before she wrote the name on the second cake. I was too late, but it's all right as it already said 'Happy Birthday Sharon.' You may purchase this one, and we will decorate another one for our order."

As I walked out of the bakery with the large cake box in my arms, I caught a glimpse of Sharon's face pressed up against the car window with a worried frown. Seeing the big box, a smile broke out. Later in a restaurant where we had the party, Mother and I continued to marvel. It was the best-tasting cake we had ever eaten. However Sharon wasn't amazed. "I knew God would give me a birthday cake," she declared.

3 year old Sharon.

Part Two: A Vision is Formed

Location of Indigeneous Tribes in Colombia

Chapter 27

Colombia Calls

The entire trip to Montana, and especially the incident of Sharon's birthday cake, had increased my faith immeasurably. I felt that if God cared enough to provide a special birthday cake, complete with name, for a little three-year-old girl out in the middle of Montana, one should not hesitate to trust Him for anything.

A number of the ladies from the prayer group were now attending services out at Bethany Fellowship on the Minnesota River, and they started inviting me to conference sessions. My hunger to know more of this victorious Christian life, and to fellowship with these godly people was so strong that I braved the Minnesota snow and cold on many a dark winter evening. Russell often accompanied me while Chad stayed at home with the younger children. One night in a small blizzard, Russell and I got stuck in a snow bank. I wondered how long the gas in the tank would keep our heater running; however after a short wait, along came two "Good Samaritans" who shoveled us out. I wanted to attend Bethany on Sundays as well, but Chad thought we should remain in our other church. There had been two church "splits," and he hoped that by staying in the church we could bring all our friends back together again.

Part Two: A Vision is Formed

I soon became acquainted with the well-stocked bookstore at Bethany, which specialized in "Deeper Life" and missionary materials. For some time now Chad and I had been setting aside twenty per cent of our income for Christian use. A tithe went directly to our church, but another tithe was set apart in a special account so that we always had funds to give to missionaries, invest in our various young people's projects, or purchase Christian literature as the Lord might direct.

After our return from Montana, I started seeking the Lord seriously to see whether or not He was calling us to the mission field. A large obstacle was the attitude of our parents. My dad was firmly convinced that outside of the Anglo-Saxon countries, no one was supposed to be "saved" in this dispensation. When confronted with stories of conversions in other countries, he grudgingly admitted that in the goodness of God there could be some exceptions. "Also," he would mumble under his breath, "who knows; those stories are probably just fiction." When pressed, he would declare that since God knew by His foreknowledge who would be saved anyway, missionary work was superfluous. Mother more or less concurred with Dad's opinion. One thing was sure— neither wanted their children and grandchildren to move very far away from them.

On the other hand, Chad's parents were most unhappy with our church involvement as it was. They wanted us to spend weekends with them at their lake cabin north of the Twin Cities. Outside of an occasional Sunday afternoon spent at the cabin, we rarely saw them, especially as sometime during this era, Chad's mother retired from her job, and they sold their home in Minneapolis and moved permanently to the country. They wanted us to move closer to them, at least to a northern suburb of the Twin Cities, and we didn't even dare to broach the subject of going to a foreign country. At one point I had decided that we were free of any missionary obligation because of our parents' attitudes (Matt. 15:5-7), but now it seemed as though everything needed to be reevaluated.

At one time, Chad and I had decided that our former intense interest in missions had come so that we could direct young people to the foreign field and also raise our own children with a missionary vision. Now, in the light of Russell's prayer and my new relationship with the Lord, it seemed like we needed to know where we stood on this issue.

One afternoon after we were back in our little house in Bloomington, I was preparing a missionary lesson for Children's Church. I was condensing a fascinating story of missionary adventure in a jungle tribe in Ecuador. At one point a missionary family had to leave their little home in the jungle and slog through muddy trails by foot and mule as the missionary airplane that serviced them had crashed, and the mother was expecting a baby in the not too far distant future. While deeply sympathetic and impressed with the struggles of the family as they traveled the muddy jungle trail, I was suddenly overwhelmed with a strong desire to slog through mud for the Lord. The emotion was so overwhelming that I got down on my knees by the sofa and sobbed and sobbed, telling the Lord that if I could only have the privilege of someday traversing muddy trails for Him, I would be delighted.

Another day I was reading from a book by Oswald Chambers that had been loaned to me by one of the ladies from the prayer group. He spoke of the call of God going out through all the world like the broadcasting of a radio station. The voice of God was saying, "Whom shall I send, and who will go for us?" (Isaiah 6:8). Most people don't even hear the call because they don't have their spiritual radio turned on. However for the person who hears the call, the only response to make is the same as that made by the prophet Isaiah, "Here am I, Lord; send me!" Once again, I dropped down on my knees by the sofa and told the Lord that I was hearing His call and was now, at last, willing to be sent.

Part Two: A Vision is Formed

During the years that we attended the Bethesda church in Minneapolis, Chad and I heard much about a single lady missionary who was working in the country of Colombia. She was contacting a number of different Indian tribes out in the eastern plains and jungles. Excerpts from her newsletters were often read from the pulpit, and the pastor was very impressed with her manner of doing missionary work. To my delight, in the Bethany bookstore, I discovered an entire book written by this missionary and illustrated with her own sketches. It was the sort of book that once started, could not be put down, and as soon as I finished it, I mailed it off to Chad in Montana.

Sophie Meuller

As a young single woman, Sophie Meuller, had entered Colombia as the first person in her mission, an organization which specialized in seeking out unreached tribal peoples. The door to the country closed behind her, but since Sophie was already in, out into the jungles she went, looking for new tribes to evangelize. Carrying only one change of clothing, a can of powdered milk, a jar of vitamin pills, a bowl and a spoon, she traveled among eight tribes, holding lit-

Christian Indians arrive for a conference carrying their village banner.

eracy classes and evangelizing. When she went into a village, she gave her bowl to a likely-looking woman and told her to fill it with whatever she was serving her family. This way Sophie was spared the time-consuming bother of cooking, washing dishes, etc. Sometimes the most interesting delicacies appeared in the bowl, some of the most exotic being boa constrictor meat and turtle eggs. In order to prevent malnutrition, she inconspicuously drank a little powdered milk each day and took a vitamin tablet.

Jungle Indians at a Christian conference.

At the beginning of her ministry, she had mastered the Curipaco language, developed an alphabet and reading materials to teach them to read. Since she was an artist, she drew her own flannel graph characters to illustrate Bible sto-

Many hammocks are hung under a roof.

ries. She emphasized in her book how important it was to draw the characters with the right looks on the faces, putting kindly, happy, loving looks on the good characters and ugly scowls on the bad ones. Since these small jungle tribes spoke related languages and intermarried, she branched out into other tribes, using bilingual Curipacos as interpreters. By the time she extended her ministry to the outlying tribes, she sometimes had to go through two or three interpreters. (Later investigation showed that this ministry was more solid the closer you got linguistically to the Curipaco language.) Sophie Meuller continued her active ministry with the Indians right up until shortly before she died in her nineties.

Sophie Meuller

Sophie was convinced that in order to really reach the people, it was important to be poorer than they were. One day an angry dog tore a long rip in one leg of her slacks (That is what we called ladies' pants in those days.) A kindly Indian woman undertook to repair the damage, realizing that Sophie only possessed two pairs of slacks and two blouses. The woman commiserated with Sophie in her poverty. She at least owned three or four dresses. The reoccurring theme of the book was: "Why doesn't someone come and help me!"

If this book impacted me, it impacted Chad even more. He returned from Montana convinced that we should go and help. I can remember him mumbling how that I could take one or two children and go down one river, while he took the others and went down another one. I almost chickened out again at hearing that plan, but somehow I managed to hold steady. We still didn't mention anything about missionary work to our parents.

One day Chad came home from work tremendously excited. Across his desk had come an announcement of a job opportunity in the country of Colombia. The entire family would be moved to Bogotá, the capital of Colombia, furniture would be shipped etc. Chad would be in charge of a huge mapping project and would be flown all over Colombia by helicopter. The salary was excellent with an added bonus for overseas work. Chad lost no time in applying.

Now we were forced to broach the subject with our parents. Even though we didn't call it missionary work, and the financial rewards would be great, all four of our parents were opposed. They didn't want us that far away from Minneapolis. I mentioned this opportunity at the ladies' prayer meet-

A view of downtown Bogota around 1960.

Part Two: A Vision is Formed

ing the next Tuesday. They saw the offer as a wonderful opportunity to get our shipping charges paid to Colombia, but they couldn't see much opportunity for missionary work, especially to reach Indians.

A few weeks later, Chad came home from work quite dejected. His application had been refused. For the first time in his engineering career, he had been rejected. He finally admitted that he did not possess the required experience for the position, but he had thought he would be accepted anyway. It was quite a blow, but we started to get used to the idea that we were not going to Colombia. Once again we decided that the missionary vision must not have been for us, but rather that we were to be used to challenge the young people of the church to go to the mission field.

Another view of Bogota in the 1960's.

Chapter 28

No Connections?

"Let's start right here. Why aren't you folks on the mission field?"

The nerve of this man, I thought. Why, he hasn't gotten more than a step inside of the front door.

We continued to challenge the young people of the church with the call to mission. With the pastor's permission, Chad had invited a dynamic speaker from the same mission board as Sophie Mueller to address the congregation on Sunday morning. We knew from reading their literature that they believed everyone should be on the foreign field according to the Great Commission in Mark 16:15, unless the Lord especially called one to stay at home. We expected a resounding challenge to the young people that they would not be able to ignore.

Chad picked the speaker up at the Minneapolis-St. Paul airport and brought him to our home for supper and to spend the night. On the way home, he told him about the young people's group that we were working with and that he wanted him to bring a strong challenge to the young people the next morning for commitment to missions. Now, here was the missionary challenging **us** the minute he got in the door.

Part Two: A Vision is Formed

"Oh, we tried to go to the mission field," responded Chad, thinking of the rejected application.

"Yes, we tried to go as government employees," I continued, "But it didn't work out. We can't go any other way; we don't have any connections." I was thinking that we didn't have any rich friends or personal connection with a sending agency.

"You don't have any connections!" exclaimed the missionary as though he couldn't believe his ears, also giving a quick glance up at our ceiling. Suddenly we realized that while we were thinking of horizontal connections — people who would support us — he meant vertical connections to the Lord. The next morning in the Sunday service, he forgot about the young people and preached directly at us, or so it seemed. After giving a number of instances of miraculous financial supply for his family in New Guinea, he deliberately misquoted Matthew 9:37, "The harvest truly is plenteous, but the *money is short.* Now anyone raised in the church knows that it isn't the money that is short, but the *laborers that are few.* The speaker went on to show that in God's program, it is never the lack of money that is the bottleneck, but the lack of willing workers. We were assured that when God calls, He also supplies. Our faith was strengthened.

Soon after this, Chad went down to Northwestern Bible Institute in downtown Minneapolis and talked with our old friend, Dr. Harry Stam, under whom we had studied missions so many years before. Together they went through the files on Colombia, but the results of their search were not encouraging. Of the ten missions having works in Colombia, only Sophie's and one other had any work among the Indians. Letters in the files revealed that the Indian territories in Colombia were under contract with the Catholic Church, and the Bishop was the civil as well as the religious authority. No evangelicals were allowed in Indian areas. (Sophie's work was strictly a one-woman affair as she and her Indian friends kept one step ahead of the authorities. On one occasion, the Indians hid her in a 55-gallon drum as their dugout canoe passed a government checkpoint.) The door to the Indians of Colombia seemed tightly closed.

By now we were so convinced that God wanted us in Colombia ministering to Indians that we were talking about just going down there, little realizing how impossible it would be. However, before that kind of talk progressed too far, my practical side surfaced again, and I wondered aloud what we would do should we ever get in touch with some Colombian Indians. How would we go about communicating with them? Then Chad remembered his desire to go to the Summer Institute of Linguistics at Grand Forks, North Dakota.

This sounded like a good, but impossible idea. It was already late in April. Russell had brought the mumps home from school, and although he was fully recovered, Big Chad, Little Chad, and Sharon were all exhibiting "fat cheeks." The doctor had ordered Big Chad to be at bed rest for two weeks to prevent complications. Chad had very little leave accumulated, and it seemed a little drastic for him to quit his job at this point. Our house expenses would continue all summer of course, and we would have to pay tuition, board and room for five people, nursery care for the three children, plus books and incidental expenses. All told, it came to about $1,000.00 that we would need.

All this time the deadline for registration was getting closer. We felt that we needed a sure sign from the Lord that this was the step we should take. One morning we especially asked the Lord to make His will clear to us. At noon that day when the mailman came, we received a copy of *Translation* magazine, the official publication of the Wycliffe Bible Translators, which at that time only came out four times a year. On the first page was a news flash: The Wycliffe Bible Translators had just signed a contract with the country of Colombia to enter their unreached Indian tribes.

We both knew that this was the sign for which we had asked.

228 Minnesota Mom in the Land of the Ancient Mother
Part Two: A Vision is Formed

Christmas 1961.

Evening prayer time.

Russell can now read the Bible Story 1962.

Chapter 29

Ka-ga-ba

I had been attending the ladies prayer meeting for almost a year now. When I had been told that these people had been asked to leave Oxboro church because they were "speaking in tongues," I had envisioned them interrupting services, babbling unintelligible gibberish in the Wednesday night prayer meetings, and possibly even rolling in the aisles in good old "Holy Roller" style. I felt as though I were now in the inner circle with these women, participating freely in their watch night prayer meetings as well, and having deep spiritual communion with several, but I had yet to witness an act of "speaking in tongues."

Occasionally I overheard some strange sounds escaping from our bedroom when Chad was having his private devotional time, but since he was under the impression that he was not to discuss the subject, I never brought it up with him. One day I decided to ask one of my close friends from the prayer group. She told me that while most of the women did have a private prayer language that they used in their own devotions, since none of them possessed the gift of interpretation, they did not use it in the meetings.

I did not want to be left out of anything good from God that was available, but I didn't know who else to ask, so I went back to the Bethany bookstore and looked through the books on the self marked *Gifts of the Spirit*. I picked out two or three and letting the children play out in the park, I sat in the car and started to carefully go through the books. In addition to the gifts of tongues and interpretation, there were fascinating chapters on divine healing, faith, miracles, and prophecy. I had never heard the likes of this before. All too soon, the children got tired of playing in the park, and I had to put the books aside and drive them home.

Later, in the privacy of my bedroom, I asked the Lord about this praying in tongues. It seemed very interesting. I tried to yield all my vocal organs to Him, and after awhile, I did start to say some strange sounds. After a bit I realized that it was just three syllables repeated over and over, ka-ga-ba, ka-ga-ba. It didn't seem to be too dramatic. After a few days there was a little more, but basically it was just ka-ga-ba. I didn't tell anyone else about it, but once in awhile after praying, I would add it to the end of my prayer. I would not know for many years what this meant.

A few days later, I heard from one of my neighbors, that another neighbor, an older woman who lived down the block, was going to have a kidney operation. Her condition seemed to be quite serious and was all the more pathetic as she had two motherless grandchildren to raise. I came home feeling very burdened for my neighbor. I got down on my knees by the sofa again and prayed with great fervor for her healing, ending with my few strange syllables. I promptly forgot the entire incident. A week or so later, I was told that the neighbor had had the surgery, but the doctor had found absolutely nothing wrong with the kidney.

Chapter 30

Money From an Unusual Source

The time was running out to apply for admission to the Summer Institute of Linguistics. Being tremendously impressed with the manner in which the Lord had directed Amy Carmichael's mission in India through the supply of funds, I had asked the Lord to supply the $30.00 needed to accompany the registration forms from an unexpected source. By this I meant that it should not just be taken from our monthly grocery money. I wanted to personally witness this miraculous phenomena of financial supply before we burned our bridges behind us and launched out into a new undertaking.

Chad was more inclined to just send the thirty dollars out of his current paycheck, but seeing how much the sign meant to me as an indication that all our future needs would be met as well, he grudgingly concurred. As the month of April drew to an end, and he and the children recovered from the mumps, he became increasingly impatient. He had not even applied yet for a leave of absence from his job, and it was most unlikely that it would be granted.

One morning in balancing the family checkbook, I discovered an error in our favor. We had $15.00 more than the balance showed. "That is an unexpected source as far as I am concerned," declared Chad. (My checkbook errors had always been in the other direction.)

"Go ahead and send in your registration form," I suggested, "There is a place to check if your wife and family are planning to come too, and they will save a place for all of us."

Russell, Sharon & Chaddy.

Six-year-old Russell had been vitally involved in all our plans and discussions. Every few days he asked if we had sent in the applications. Always we told him that we were waiting for God to send us the money. That evening Chad filled out his form, wrote the check, and the next morning took the envelope to mail on the way as he and Russell started off to town to school and to work.

After they left I occupied myself putting the kitchen in order as Little Chad and Sharon continued sleeping. My thoughts drifted back to our wedding reception twelve years before. Again I saw in my mind's eye the pastel ice cream balls rolling around on the church floor. Too bad Mother had been so quick to pay the caterer, I thought, or we might have been able to get a refund. Suddenly, I realized that it had been the money from my childhood savings account that had paid for the wedding reception.

My thoughts took another leap back in time. Now I was sitting in the huge Minneapolis Civic Auditorium. A plea was being made for funds to equip the Youth for Christ team that was going to China. I wanted to give the money in my savings account but feared my parents' disapproval. Why—that was God speaking to me way back there! I thought. Now that I was familiar with His voice, I knew that He had asked for my money. Shamefully I remembered my substitute offering of 75 cents and the praise I had received for it. No wonder that reception had been a mess, I thought.

Then my mind came back to the present. At the birth of each of my children, my parents had opened a bank account for them. Money had been added occasionally, and at the present time, each child had somewhat over twenty dollars in his account. Remembering that it had been fear of my parents' disapproval that had kept me from obeying the Lord's voice, I resolved to always maintain an atmosphere in my relationship with my own children in which they would feel free to use their money for anything the Lord should direct.

The thought was just fading from my consciousness when the telephone rang. It was Chad calling from work. "Patty, you'll never believe what happened this morning. As I put the envelope in the mailbox in front of the post office, Russell asked me why we were just sending in my registration and not yours too. I explained that God had supplied $15.00 for my application, but that we were still waiting for another $15.00 for yours. He pulled himself up to his full height and got that deep tone in his voice like he does when he wants to say something important. 'I want you to go right down to the bank,' he declared, 'and take fifteen dollars out of my savings account. I have decided to send Mother to the Institute of Linguistics this summer.' But—," and here a puzzled tone crept into Chad's voice, "We can't take the little kid's money, can we?"

Chills ran up and down my spine. I told Chad of my thoughts that morning. The next day we went down to the bank and drew out Russell's money. Solemnly, he handed me fifteen dollars and returned the rest to his account.

In short succession after our registrations were accepted, Chad was granted a three-month leave of absence from his job, we rented the house for the exact dates that we would be away, our old station wagon sold for top price to the first customer, our church gave us a going away party and a gift of $50.00, and to top it all off, the U.S. Army Reserve requested Chad's services to help with engineering problems for 15 days ending two days before classes were to start at the University, thus giving us the last $300.00 that we needed to complete the thousand.

At last we could keep our plans from our parents no longer. Mother accepted the inevitable graciously, even baking us a large tin of her special sugar cookies to take along. Because Dad had several times expressed the opinion that I should have gone on for a Master's degree instead of getting married, I stressed the fact that we would be earning graduate level credit that could later be applied to an advanced degree. Still he was disconsolate.

Chad broke the news to his own parents, and they too were most unhappy. Their frustration focused on an old oriental rug that they had loaned to us for use in our living room because they were no longer using it. "The renters will destroy your house," they grimly predicted, "We are going to remove our rug so that it won't be ruined." We wondered how the renters would react to a bare living room floor, but there was nothing more that we could do. (Actually they never did get around to removing the rug before we left for North Dakota.)

It was amazing how much equipment and baggage we deemed necessary for the three months in Grand Forks. I had always felt that Minnesota summers were much too brief and tried to pack a lot of fun and outdoor living into these few warm months. All of our summer equipment had to go with us, including the children's bicycles and Russell's accumulation of books and games. We rented a large U-haul trailer and hitched it to the Mercury. Out on the highway, we realized that the Mercury lacked the necessary power to pull the heavy trailer, but after chugging along at a slow speed for several hours, the Lord sent a strong tail wind which blew against the large expanse of trailer and effectively pushed us right up to the university of North Dakota at Grand Forks. We were ready to start our missionary training.

Chad, the civil engineer from the North Woods, and I, the Minnesota mom together, with our three children would step through that university door and start the gradual transformation of becoming foreign missionaries. We would never be the same again.

Pat and Chad in winter in Minnesota.

Sharon plays outside in the snow.

Marie Monsen.

Appendix

Marie Monsen
Norwegian Missionary
1878 – 1962

It is quite a thrill to find that you have a famous Missionary in your family history, even if she is a relative by marriage on your husband's side of the family. This discovery was especially exciting as it occurred during a time of eager interest in missions, when we were seeking the Lord as to whether or not WE, Chad and I, were receiving such a call.

Marie Monsen was no ordinary missionary. She is still remembered as a "hero of the faith" in many parts of China and is known as "the Mother of the House Churches."

Early Life in Norway

Marie Monsen was born and grew up in Sandviken, just north of Bergen, Norway, in a home in which she was supplied with only the necessities of life. Her father, Johannes Monsen Midthun, was a "house-preacher." As a young girl, she loved to wander about among the mountains and hills of her native land. She trained to be a teacher but when she finished her education, she was one year too young to take the test for certification. It seems that during that time she became clear about her missionary call and was accepted by the Norwegian Lutheran China Society for work in China. She was then sent to the Lovisenberg Hospital and Training School in Oslo for further training. Here she became acquainted with a woman named Mrs. Karoline Samet, a future coworker in China, from whom we learn of Marie's early life. "It was evident from the first moment of contact with her that Miss Monsen was an unusually gifted woman." Mrs. Samet writes, "She possessed considerable originality of mind, and as a rule was never found treading the beaten paths." In those days such behavior was not always well received. Marie was noted for being always ready to take the part of those who were weak.

First Trip to China

Marie arrived in China on September 1, 1901, during the tail-end of the Boxer Rebellion (November 1899 - September 7, 1901). The uprising began as an anti-foreign, anti-imperialist, peasant-based movement by members of the Society of Right and Harmonious Fists, who were simply called "Boxers" by the Westerners. The Boxers believed that the expulsion of "foreign devils" would magically renew Chinese society and begin a new golden age. They attacked foreign-

ers who were building railroads as well as Christians, whom they held responsible for the foreign domination of China. Many Christians, both Chinese and foreign missionaries were martyred during this time. The China Inland Mission lost more members than any other missionary agency: 58 adults and 21 children were killed.

Marie got off to a slow start in her missionary career: Soon after her arrival, she fell down a stairway, which left her unconscious with a very severe concussion. Not long after this she contracted malaria, which almost proved fatal. For a long time she was not allowed to study the language because of her health, and when she did so, she made slow progress because of reoccurring malaria and severe headaches. However in the summer of 1906 she was healed through prayer. From that time on, she took the Lord as her Great Physician, and she needed His help on more than one occasion. She was also used throughout her life in the impartation of miracles of divine healing and other signs and wonders.

She soon realized that most conversions among the Chinese were very superficial and many times based on a desire for education and western culture, rather than a real surrender of the life to the Lord. She also saw the need for revival, and that it could only come by overcoming prayer. She and some of her women coworkers were very impressed by the revival that came to Korea in 1907, and pled in prayer that a similar revival could take place in China, although some influential male missionary leaders felt that such an occurrence in China was not possible.

Marie felt the desire to travel to Korea to "bring back some burning coals of revival" to her own field. She thought of praying for the money to make the trip. As she prayed, a definite word came to her: What you want from that journey, you may be given right where you are in answer to prayer. She gave her solemn pledge to pray until she received it.

The first time she set herself to walk across her room to her prayer place to fulfill her pledge; she was spiritually attacked by what she can only describe as a boa constrictor. It wound its coils around her and was squeezing the life out of her. Finally, while gasping for breath, she was able to groan out, "Jesus! Jesus! Jesus!" Each time she uttered the name, the coils loosened, and finally the "serpent" left. Her first conscious thought was "If that prayer means so much, then my promise to pray must be kept by all means." That experience sustained her for the almost twenty years that were to pass before the first stirrings of revival began in China.

Second Trip to China

Her first term of service was deemed "disastrous," and she returned to Norway in 1909, however in 1911, she returned to China again. There is very little information about this second trip to China. I believe that this was the time in which she learned the language and made accurate and original evaluations of the missionary work among the Chinese that would later lead to her unique ministry. In 1922, she returned to Norway again.

Third Trip to China

Marie went out to China again in 1926 or 1927. This was right when the communists were first starting to make trouble. It was during this third trip to China that she was instrumental in what became known as the "Shantung revival." It seems that everywhere she went on this, her third trip; God used her in a marvelous way to revive the churches.

Straight away the Chinese believers knew there was something different about this missionary. Whereas most of the others preached about God's love and acceptance, Marie told the church leaders they were all hypocrites. In the words of one present-day house church leader, "Marie Monsen didn't speak smooth words to impress the people. Instead, she brought fire from the altar of God. The people were struck to the heart with God's conviction, were sickened by their sin, and revival broke out." She insisted that they, themselves, must be radically born-again in order to enter the Kingdom of Heaven. She often interviewed pastors and church leaders asking them to tell her about when they were "born again." They usually hesitated and she would add, "Tell me about when you were first one person, and then became another person. That is what it means to be born again." The amazed pastors were sent to their rooms with Bible verses to study and to spend time in prayer and come back again when they were "born again." After varying amounts of time, they would come back to her with shining faces and a strong testimony of their new birth. After that, their preaching would take off with great power.

Many came to see her and confess their sins, but she often sent them away, some as often as three to four times. They were not yet in a condition of real need. "Pray that God's Spirit may enlighten you concerning your sins," was the admonition she gave them. She never tired of admonishing the other missionaries, "Do not gather unripe fruit."

Marie Monsen's life-style matched her words. She was fearless, traveling thousands of miles through bandit-infested territory to share the Gospel, and she showed great faith, love, and courage wherever she went. On one occasion Marie and some Chinese Christians were in a city that was being looted by the Chinese Army. They heard shooting and shouting all night, but no soldier came to bang on their door. Terrified neighbors climbed over their walls to take refuge with them. As the bullets whistled overhead, Marie shared with all of them the comfort in the words of Psalm 91:5 "You will not fear the terror of the night, nor the arrow that flies by day." In her own words she substituted "bullets" for "arrows." The Psalm goes on to say that the Lord will send angels to keep His people safe.

The following morning, many of the other people who lived around the compound came to ask who their "protectors" were. At first Marie was not sure what they meant; until she heard the same account from so many that she knew it was true. All these reports were that they had seen three tall foreign soldiers standing on the high roof of their Gospel Hall, one at each end, and one in the middle. A fourth protector was sitting on the porch over the main gate, keeping watch in every direction. They were there all night, and all the accounts said they "shone." Neither Marie nor any of her Christian friends had seen them. Only the nonbelievers living nearby had seen these angel protectors to convince them that God takes care of all who trust in Him.

Marie's life was unusually rich in experiences. Money never appealed to her as of being of any worth. She was always willing to extend help to such as were in need. *Prove me now herewith, saith Jehovah of Hosts, if I will not open you the windows of heaven.* Marie did this, and she never came to grief. "She went to steamships without money to buy a ticket; she traveled by rail across the United States without provisions; she made a journey to the Northland without a steamer berth. At one time when she was suffering from hunger, this verse came to her, *Your Father knoweth what things ye have need of.* She was led to a loaded table without the payment of money, and afterwards was in a position to help a fellow traveler who was on his way to tell his mother that there is no God. She always stuck to the promises, and God never failed her. But to surrender everything unconditionally into the hand of God is not a lesson that is learned in one day. She had to go through deep waters to come to the place of utter dependence on God.

One of her contemporaries wrote: "As a co-worker she was always sympathetic and considerate, and on the whole, easy to get along with. Her aim was to go the way of the Lord and do His errands, so (even in China) it was never a question of her following the beaten paths. Consequently, there were times when some stood wondering and questioning, but that it has paid her to follow the way of the Lord and to be in His will has been amply shown by her life during recent years."

Of all the amazing missionary experiences that were granted to Marie Monsen, the one that stands out is the story of her 23 days in which she was a captive of pirates who held a ship on which she was traveling to hold meetings in Shantung. Since Shantung was in hot country, Marie had packed all her belongings, including her warm clothing, and put them in storage. Since she only planned to be on the ship one night, she traveled light with no bedding or sweater. At the last moment before she left for her trip, a package was delivered to her from Norway. Somehow it had been delayed. Marie was quite annoyed by this extra baggage, but there was nothing else to do but take it all along with her. Just before boarding the ship, for some reason unknown to her, she bought a bag of apples from a vendor. Now she was really loaded down with hand baggage, and she berated herself for having purchased the apples. Then, as a last straw, she boarded the ship and found that no cabin had been assigned to her.

This story has been published several times in books by different titles, *A Wall of Fire, We Are Escaped,* and others. The following is from an account published by the Overseas Missionary Fellowship in a book entitled *The Obstinate Horse and Other Stories.*

Pirate Ship – Yellow Sea Journey

> MARIE MONSEN looked round her "cabin" with a rueful smile. It was little bigger than a cupboard, had bare boards for a bed, no window, and was thick with dust. All the other cabins were filled, and as this one, belonging to the Mate, had been offered to her, she gladly accepted it.
>
> "It is only for one night," she thought. She was the only white-skinned person on board, though there were several hundred Chinese passengers. Having seen her suitcases safely put in the cabin, she went out on deck to talk to her fellow-passengers and to give out leaflets which told the Gospel in a simple way for those who had never heard it. As darkness fell, she went to her cabin, knelt in prayer by her hard bed, and then lay down, fully clothed, to sleep. She felt sure that God meant her to make this journey because she had prayed much about it.
>
> Very early next morning she was startled by the sound of pistol shots, the shrieks of passengers, doors

Part Two: A Vision is Formed

being wrenched open, and people running up and down. Twenty pirates had mingled with the passengers and, once at sea, compelled the captain at pistol point to change course. Now the passengers were being ordered out of their cabins down to the hold.

"Oh dear," thought Marie, "How awful! Pirates!" Immediately she remembered a verse in the Bible that had often been a comfort to her in times of danger. She repeated it to herself in this way.

"Fear not, Marie, for I am with you; be not dismayed, Marie, for I am your God; I will strengthen you, Marie, yes, I will uphold you with my victorious right hand." And then she added, "Lord, I will obey and not be afraid."

The pirates came to her cabin one after another and ordered her down to the hold, but as they never stopped to see their orders carried out, she stayed where she was. "God gave me this cabin," she said to herself, "so here I shall stay."

A second lot of sixty pirates came aboard with guns and ammunition. They broke the lock of Marie's door and came in and out freely. Her only defense was prayer. One of the leaders held a pistol at her head, saying, "I'll shoot you!"

"No, you can't shoot me just when you like," she replied. Somehow all her fear had been taken away. "My God has said, 'No weapon that is formed against thee shall prosper.'"

Again and again in the days that followed, Marie heard him say, "Just think! She says I can't shoot her whenever I like because her God says that no weapon that is formed against her shall prosper." One man stole her wrist watch, but surprisingly, a man who seemed to have some sort of authority and was more friendly to her than any of the others ordered it to be returned to her.

On the second day Marie noticed that the cabin had fittings for an inner screen door. If only she could have that door! There seemed to be only one of the real crew about, so when he brought her small allowance of hot drinking water she asked him if he knew where it was. "Yes," he replied, "and when the pirates are smoking their opium I will bring it up." He did so, and helped Marie to fix it in position. How wonderful it was to have some air, and yet to be able to fasten her door again on the inside!

For five days the ship, under its new command, steamed up and down, shooting at every boat that came in sight, and then capturing and looting them. Marie's cabin was situated between the pirates' headquarters on the one side and the ammunition store on the other. Day and night pandemonium reigned. After five days Marie was utterly exhausted from the noise and lack of sleep. But there was nothing to do but pray! "Lord, let me sleep. I ask You for sleep." Miraculously, the ship suddenly became quiet and Marie fell sound asleep. After the ship had anchored in a secluded estuary out of sight, it was never so noisy again.

About this time Marie's friends had heard that the ship had fallen into the hands of pirates and were praying earnestly for her. And their prayers were heard. From that time on, instead of feeling as if she were swimming against the stream, it was as if she were being borne along on a strong current to a safe landing.

After looting the passengers' clothing, the pirates paraded up and down outside Marie's cabin in fine silk garments, looking very ridiculous. For a few days they all wore spectacles too! New bicycles from the hold also provided hours of entertainment, as one after another tried to ride them up and down the narrow deck.

This deck was the place, too, where the pirates chose to have their meals consisting of all sorts of luxuri-

Part Two: A Vision is Formed

ous tinned foods they had stolen. They often offered some to Marie, who replied,

"No, thank you!"

"Well, tell us what you would like to eat, and we will try and get it for you."

"No, thank you! I can't eat stolen food; and whatever I asked for, you would only go and steal from other people."

"But you will die of starvation," they said.

"No, my Father in Heaven is able to keep me alive," she answered. And this is how her Heavenly Father fed Marie.

She had bought some apples the day before she sailed with-out really knowing why, and she had been given four boxes of chocolates. These with a few biscuits were all the food she had, so she divided it up into rations to last for nine days. The nine days had passed, the food was gone, and there was still no hope of being freed. But Marie was not worried, just interested to see how the Lord was going to supply her need now!

On the tenth morning before it was light, there was a gentle scratching on Marie's door. She had been thinking of the story of Elijah and the ravens, and as she jumped down from her bunk she said to herself, "This is the raven!" It was the Mate whom she had not seen since they sailed.

"Have you any food?" he whispered.

"No, I haven't," she truthfully replied.

"Let me come in then. The guard is on the other side of the ship. I have a box full of eggs here in my cabin and a tin of cakes. You can have them all. I bought them in Tientsin with my own honestly earned money." Saying this, he pulled out the treasure from among the buckets of paint, old shoes, empty paraffin tins, and other junk. Every day he appeared at that early hour, took four eggs, boiled them, and brought them back to her. Her daily ration became four eggs and two sweet cakes, and the supply lasted out until they were rescued. Marie was never hungry.

The weather was stormy and bitterly cold, and Marie had brought no bedding. As she was going to a warmer part of the country and expected to spend only one night at sea, she had packed all her winter clothes. But God knew what she would need and had made provision beforehand. Just before she started out, a belated Christmas parcel had arrived containing a warm cardigan and woolen stockings. The post that day had also brought no less than five fat bundles of newspapers from home. "Oh, dear," she had sighed, "why didn't these things come earlier? I shall have to take them with me now, and my baggage will be heavier." How glad she was of that warm cardigan! The newspapers came in very useful too, for, pinned inside her coat, they helped to keep her warm at nights.

The days dragged by. More than two weeks had already gone. An intense desire filled Marie's heart that the hundreds of passengers and the thirty-five members of the crew, all of them heathen, might see that hers was a living Almighty God.

Often one or other of the pirates said to her, "Don't you know you are worth a lot of money?" —showing that they hoped to get a good ransom for her. Sometimes they deliberately tried to make her impatient, usually by saying they meant to keep her captive for a long time.

"Don't you ever get impatient?" they would ask her.

"Do I look impatient?"

"No, that's just what you don't look. Whatever we do, we can't provoke you. Aren't you longing to go ashore and get away from us?"

Part Two: A Vision is Formed

"No, I'm not, and I thank God for that. He sent me to China to preach the Gospel, and now He wants me here to preach the Gospel to you, so I'll stay as long as God wants. It is He who has allowed this to happen."

"Can you understand such peace?" she heard them say to each other. "We can see it in her face. The other passengers look quite different. They get more and more impatient every day!"

Nearly three weeks had passed. Then government gunboats were reported to be nearby, and preparations were made to flee with the loot. About fifty junks, moored alongside the ship, were loaded with food and other stolen goods. But the great question concerned Marie and what to do with her. For hours they argued, and Marie could hear all that they were saying through the thin boards which divided her cabin from their headquarters. It was clear that only the Lord could deliver her. As she prayed He reassured her with His Word in Psalm 31:20: "Thou shalt hide them in the secret of thy presence from the pride of man: thou shalt keep them secretly in a pavilion from the strife of tongues."

Plans were finally made to leave the ship at 3 pm on the twenty-first day, but Marie was so sure that God was not going to let her be carried off that she dared to tell the pirates so!

Just before the zero hour a tremendous storm arose around the ship, causing all the junks to cast off in great haste and make for the shore. When the storm subsided Marie neither heard a sound nor saw anyone for some hours. The pirates evidently believed that it was her God who had sent the storm to protect her. But the next day they decided to go ahead with their original plans. But when their spies returned, Marie could hear loud arguments and sounds of disagreement among the leaders. Then the time for their daily opium came, and nothing more could be done that day. The day following, as they were about to leave, Marie heard one of the pirates say,

"Go and tell the foreigner to get into the junk at once. We must go!" Hearing steps on the deck, Marie jumped to her feet.

"Lord, what will You do now?" she breathed.

The door was flung open and a pirate faced Marie. He stood staring for a long time, but without speaking a word; nor did he cross the threshold. Then, without delivering his message, he slammed the door and went off. Marie heard him say, "You can do what you like to me, but I can't give your order!"

That evening an unexpected chance came for Marie to talk to the pirates about Christ for two or three hours.

"We are bad, only bad," said one. "We were born bad. We do evil from morning to night and from night to morning. You were born good. You don't hate us like the other passengers."

"Yes," they all agreed, "that is quite true." To which Marie replied that she was born with the same evil heart as they, and went on to tell them of the Saviour who came to save all men and give them new hearts. They were clearly impressed, for they listened to her in complete silence. It was an evening they would never forget.

Next day was Sunday, the twenty-third day of Marie's captivity. Just after noon the sound of distant gunfire was heard, and after much running about, most of the pirates left the ship. Those left released the Captain from his cabin and ordered him to take the ship up the estuary. But it was too late. A gunboat was hard on their heels. In the cabin next door Marie heard fragments of a conversation:

"We must take the foreigner with us. . . they won't dare to shoot if they see we have her. . . but how can we? She would have to run, and after eating nothing for twenty-three days, she couldn't walk, much less

Part Two: A Vision is Formed

run." Marie thought she recognized the voice of the friendly pirate who had returned her watch.

"Hurry! Hurry! There's no time to lose," shouted someone; and with that, the last of the pirates left the ship.

Marie, her heart full of thankfulness, was soon out of her cabin. Looking out over the water, she saw some of the pirates already on shore in full flight, littering the path with discarded garments as they ran. Others were making for the shore as fast as they could in the boats.

Seeing this, Marie ran down to the hold where the passengers were imprisoned, shouting, "Come up! Come up! The pirates have all gone!" But no one stirred. Again she shouted down to them, "I am the foreigner. The pirates really have all gone. Come up and see." Cautiously they emerged and when they saw their former captors fleeing pell-mell across the sands, they forgot their usual Chinese dignity and laughed and cried and embraced one another. Then, rather sheepishly, they apologized to Marie.

"Forgive us, please. You see we have been sitting with a sword pointed at our hearts for twenty-three days!"

The original voyage southwards was now resumed without the unwelcome fellow-passengers. So Marie had four more days on that ship to witness to God's faithfulness. The other travelers said to her, "Your great God has helped you, but none of our small gods has helped us!" This was Marie's great opportunity to speak of the One who is "our refuge and strength, a very present help in trouble" and of the Saviour who can also rescue us from our sins and set us free (Psalm 46:1).

Ministry in Manchuria

Instead of taking her to Shantung as she had planned, the ship left her in Manchuria. This was a Danish mission field, and Marie had visited it once before. On her first visit, some years before, the leaders and especially the national Christians had regarded her as a representative of interior China who had both the accent and the manners of the south. A frank Manchu Christian actually told her, "Our missionaries speak our language." The Manchus were of a different race, taller than the Chinese and proud of their national traits.

On this second visit, however, it was very different. Marie had come straight from captivity among pirates, and the Manchu Christians had been praying together with their missionaries for her release. When, at their own request, she recounted to them the experience she had gone through; it was as though a separating wall between them fell.

Marie found joy in meeting many of the Danish missionaries whose intense desire was to see the Holy Spirit work in the churches. One of the Danish missionaries, whom we shall call Christina, said what many must have thought; that even before leaving Denmark for the mission field, she had a strong impression that the Christians of the New Testament were one kind of Christian, and we of today quite another kind. The sense of difference had become even more marked since she came to Manchuria. Christina said that instead of what she longed and prayed for, she had met with only humiliation, loneliness, and discouragement, as though God had no use for her. True He had not rejected her from being His child, but He surely could not have her in His service. She had not even the courage to face taking back her teaching post at home in Denmark. She thought she might be able to work on the land, not among souls at all, not realizing that the Lord was emptying her in order to fill her.

Marie discovered that many other missionaries felt the same. This state of mind was indeed one of the conditions that made revival possible, "that no flesh should glory before God." Christina, who was in such despair, said afterwards that for her the path led on through I Cor. 1:27 *God hath chosen the foolish things of the world to confound the wise; and God hath chosen the weak things of the world to confound the things that are mighty; and the base things of the world, and things that are despised, hath God chosen, yea, and things that are not, to bring to naught things that are.* Also Rom. 8:17a, If *children, then heirs; heirs of God and joint-heirs with Christ.* And Gal. 3:13, 14, *Christ hath redeemed us from the curse of the law, being made a curse for us: for it is written, Cursed is every one that hangeth on a tree: that the blessing of Abraham might come on the Gentiles through Jesus Christ, and that we might receive the promise of the Spirit through faith.* Christina received these words by faith and with an inward assurance, which the Lord confirmed to her about three months later. She was granted the privilege of continuous reaping for the next ten years, instead of having to face the grievous fact that there was nothing for her to do but go back to Denmark a failure, unfit even for the least ministry among human souls.

Among these Danish missionaries, Marie found some, who like herself, never could put away from their minds the thoughts of what the Spirit of God had done in Korea. It had helped them to hold on in prayer, hoping against hope, although dogged by their own sense of failure. It was in the wise counsel of God that Marie was set ashore at Dalny in Manchuria after the twenty-three days of captivity.

Ministry at Peitaiho and Chefoo

The Lord worked mightily through Marie in Manchuria and then sent her to Peitaiho, a well known health resort in northeast China on the sea. Here hundreds of missionaries gathered each summer to hear speakers from England and the USA. To Marie's surprise and dismay, a telegram came inviting her to Peitaiho and also to minister there. Her train was late, and a very smartly dressed American picked her up at the train station. He took one look at "dowdy me" in Marie's own words and decided he had no use for her. Marie felt like a sparrow among herons. One of the great missionary leaders took it upon himself to "clip the wings of the sparrow." He sat in the front during her messages. It felt to Marie as if he had turned into a "mighty Himalayan mountain over which the message could not pass to reach the crowd of missionaries behind him." Intercessory prayer was made, and the "mountain" started to melt. Each day it seemed less formidable. One day he greeted her outside the meeting hall and told her that her messages were being used of God to bless his soul. Before the conference was over, he was inviting Marie to share prayer times with him according to Matt. 18:19 *"If two of you shall agree on earth as touching anything that they shall ask, it shall be done for them of my Father which is in heaven.*

In the autumn of 1929, from Peitaiho Marie went to Chefoo, another place by the sea in northeast China. The China Inland Mission had three schools for the children of their missionaries there, as well as a hospital and sanitarium. This spot became a natural holiday resort for missionaries. Marie had been there before and had enjoyed intensive prayer fellowship with like-minded missionaries who longed for a revival such as Korea was experiencing. It was a joy for Marie to once more visit these dear missionaries with a heart for revival, most of them Americans.

After the first few days of meetings, one of the American woman missionaries "fell sick." This woman, whom we shall call Emily, was regarded as one of the best in the whole mission. Though none of the others knew until later, Emily had spent the night in getting right with God and of being brought through to salvation quite alone in her room. After the morning meeting, she asked to be allowed to give her testimony to the large audience. Her testimony was deeply moving. After the meeting was over, the missionaries gathered around Emily and asked for an explanation of what looked to them to be an incredible situation. How was it that she had not experienced salvation until now?

They were told that Emily herself was the only one that could answer that question, and she proceeded to do so quite simply. Because she had raised her hand in response to an appeal in an evangelistic meeting, she was led to believe that this was the great decision, but she had not received life. But now, after her night of dealing with God and man (she had written letters to her home in the USA), and then by faith she had received Jesus, God's unspeakable gift, relying on John 1:12 *"As many as received him, to them gave he power to become the sons of God, even to them that believe on his name."*

An elderly missionary then said, deeply moved: "I remember the experiences of my student days were just like this. We had revival then. Perhaps this is the beginning?" Marie realized that he meant that he had not seen revival since. His deep emotion touched all his fellow-workers, and the sense of strain that had come with Emily's testimony passed in a moment.

Marie's Messages

From Chefoo Marie continued her journey to many places, eventually reaching Shantung, her previous destination before her capture. Everywhere she ministered, souls were born anew, many of them being among the church leaders and members. We may well ask, "What were the messages preached by Miss Monsen that brought such revival to the churches?" Gustav Carlberg writes in his book, *China in Revival:* He and his co-laborers heard more and more news of the blessings surrounding Marie's ministry. Was she not one of their own? Why should others be revived, while there in her own Norwegian Lutheran Mission, they were praying and longing for revival. "With every letter from Miss Monsen, our prayers received a new impetus and became more intense as the time went on, until finally they were in the nature of distress calls. Then the news reached us that she would be with us at our annual conference at Chenping. There was a general feeling of expectancy as we journeyed to this meeting, and we were not disappointed in our expectations. It was a never-to-be-forgotten experience to have her in our midst again.

"Already at this meeting, it became clear to us that God had fashioned Miss Monsen into a seasoned soul winner through the experiences she had gone through in the north, and that she was in possession of a power from God that was well nigh irresistible."

Mr. Carlberg goes on to give us a glimpse of Marie's preaching:

"The first text she used was from the third chapter of John, *Ye must be born anew.* The greater part of this address consisted in short questions, cast forth with holy, penetrating seriousness: 'Why are you a Christian? Is it not that you wish to enter heaven? What does Jesus say here? *Except ye be born anew, ye cannot enter the Kingdom of God.* **Ye cannot! Ye cannot!**' These words sank like lead into the hearts of the listeners.

"The next text was from Rev. 20:12, about the sins that were written in the books with such clearness. 'Also in Jer. 17:1, we see that your sins are written **with a pen of iron** on the tablets of flesh in your hearts so that no one can erase them.'

"Other texts were Mark 14:3-11, about Judas. 'He was a preacher of the gospel; he was a member of the church; he was a disciple. But he was false; he was a thief. Are you a preacher of the gospel, or are you a thief?'

"She aimed in the first place at our leaders and the workers in our congregations. She spoke from Prov. 28:13 about covering one's transgressions. **All are born with an inclination to cover their sins.** Other texts used were, Is. 59:1-

4, *Your iniquities have separated between you and your God:* Is.64:6, *Our righteousnesses are as a polluted garment*; 1 Cor. 6:9, with the question, **'Is this a catalog of your sins? Read and find out if your sins are there.'** Also Mark 7:21-23, with the same question and the same admonition.

"Then came John 1:14, *He is full of grace and truth*, 'He will not permit you to remain full of falsehood and deceit.' And Is. 1:18 'If you will only acknowledge your sins before God they **shall be as white as snow.**'

"Finally, there was an address to believers about being in the will of God. 'The unsaved have God's Will behind them. The saved have God's will before them. Some are in God's will; others are outside of it. They try to stretch God's will so as to make it conform to theirs.'

"At the end of each service, she took her place near the door, and few were those who managed to get by without having the question asked them, **'Are you saved?'**

"'**It felt like the thrust of a sword,**' they explained afterwards.

"After the next meeting, they received another sword thrust, **'Are you still on the road to destruction?'**

"After the annual meeting there was a special meeting for workers and leaders. Those who were present told of the powerful working of the Holy Spirit manifest at these meetings. During the course of the meetings Miss Monsen spent one night in prayer before she could find courage to step up to Pastor Han Liu Ging and tell him she was afraid he did not have life in God. He came under deep conviction, and after two days found release. He said afterwards that there was something that melted within him when she took him aside. He felt the love of God was impelling her and that he must give in. Later on, he became Miss Monsen's helper during a series of meetings and is one among those God has used to further the revival.

"Miss Monsen's plan was first to destroy the false security of the church members. She spoke of the various kinds of patches the unsaved used to hide behind when they tried to persuade themselves they were saved. Then she spoke of sin, one sin at a time. It had cost her several days of prayerful struggle before she became willing, as she expressed it, to 'descend into the miry cesspool of sin' in connection with the sixth commandment against adultery. But it turned out that one of Satan's well-nigh impregnable strongholds was at last broken into when this particular sin was brought out into the open.

"Another text that was laid heavily on her consciousness was, *It is a fearful thing to fall into the hands of the living God.* People by means of this text were placed face to face with God. Finally the words of gracious promise from the Scriptures came as balm on open sores. 'Unless He, who was without sin, had been made sin for us, God could never have said to the sinner, 'Come, when you are in earnest about your sins, God . . . will speak words of comfort to your heart.'

"At each series of meetings, there was no pronounced movement or great visible result. She was ever alert to hinder strong emotional outburst or public confession. Everything was done quietly. After she was gone, it became evident that God's Spirit had plowed deep furrows. We could begin to gather in the harvest of souls."

Marie makes it very clear in her writings that this revival was the result of faithful, unrelenting prayer. At one time she was granted her desire to travel to Korea and learn of the beginnings of the Korean revival. Here is the story in her own words, "It was a never-to-be forgotten day when the desire of twenty-three years was granted, and I stood at last in the room—the very crucible—where the missionaries had met daily to pray. Here they were stripped of all that was of self, till they were "unprofitable servants" in their own eyes and 'declared themselves bankrupt.' Here they unitedly resolved to continue in prayer until they were given a revival like the revival in Wales and in India. Their request was granted."

Part Two: A Vision is Formed

A Chinese elder who had worked for many years in a large church with a vast surrounding district made this observation, "To think that we have seen all this here on earth, seen the Spirit of God break and mold the hardest, most hopeless hearts, so that they see themselves and condemn themselves. It is almost too good for us to be living in it all."

Marie continues, "All the time it was simply walking in prepared works, and work is not burdensome then, even when days are long and half the night is given for service as well. It was like living on the heights where it is easy to breathe. That must have been how John Wesley, for instance, was able to ride all over England and sometimes hold as many as five meetings a day.

"There was wonderful fellowship among these missionaries in Korea who had been welded together in prayer and between the missionaries and the Chinese Christians. 'The Spirit of God has made a new little world for us through this (revival),' said a radiant Chinese leader."

Marie Leaves China for the Last Time

In 1932, Marie left China for the last time. She arrived at Los Angeles, California on the 27th of April, aboard the Tatsuta Maru, which had set sail from Kobe, Japan. On the ship manifest, she lists her sister, Mrs. C.M. Stendal, as her closest living relative and her final destination as Norway. It seems that she stayed with the Stendals in Minneapolis for a while before continuing on to Norway. The C.M. Stendals were the owners of the largest shoe store in Minneapolis, located on a choice corner of the downtown area. When I was growing up in south Minneapolis, "C.M Stendal, the Shoeist," was a well-known name. The three floors of high quality shoes for men and women at the Stendal store were a "must-have" for teachers, professional people, and the high society of Minneapolis and St. Paul. I believe the Stendals also catered to folks with special needs in their footwear.

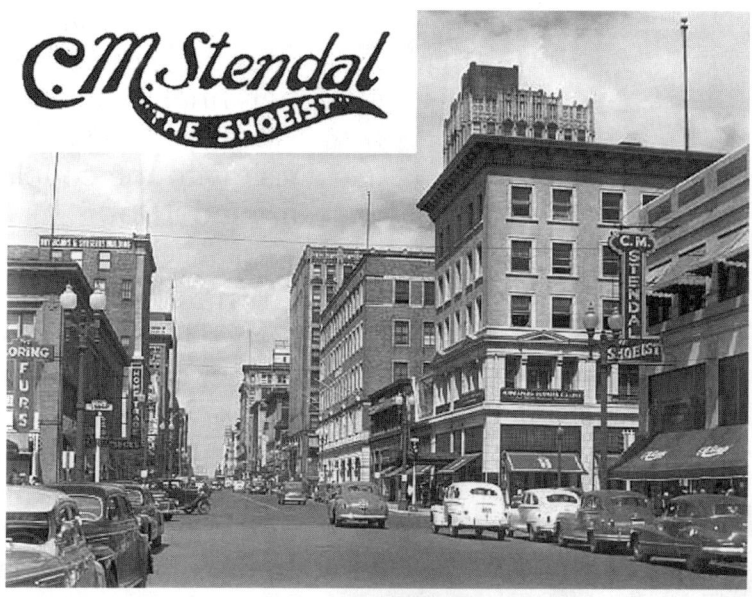

Minneapolis 1947.

When I first met my husband, Chad, he proudly told me, "Lets drive downtown and look at my name in lights." His parents had carefully named him, their only child, with a similar name as that of their wealthy, childless uncle with the not too well-veiled hopes that their offspring might someday become the inheritor of the supposed Stendal fortune. They thought it might help to give him the initials that their uncle had made famous. Chad worked as a stock boy at the shoe store during his high school years, but his conversion to Christ at age 18, and his being drafted into the US Army almost immediately thereafter turned his life in a different direction. When he was pursuing his career as a civil engineer before the Lord called us into missionary service, we visited the C.M. Stendals several times. On one occasion, Chad tried to "witness" to his elderly relatives. Mr. C.M. quickly cut him off with the remark that words like that should only be spoken inside a church. Mrs. C.M. was a little more receptive, "Remember dear," she gently reminded him, "This is the same thing that Marie was telling us." As far as we know, Marie

Part Two: A Vision is Formed

C.M. Stendal & wife Bertha Monsen Midthun, circa 1960.

Monsen only visited the Stendals once, during her final return trip to Norway in 1932. Our visit with the couple was around 1960.

It was well known in China that Marie returned to Norway to care for her elderly parents. It is unclear if she ever planned to return to China, but at any rate she would have been unable to do so after China was closed to foreign missionaries. It has been said that her work in China was completed.

Marie's Planting Becomes a Harvest

Many years later in the province of Honan, a Chinese pastor stated, "We have traveled through several provinces to summer conferences for the deepening of the spiritual life and have come home with our ulcers of sin a little scratched on the surface, but this time (in the meetings of Marie Monsen) we have had treatment that went to the root of the trouble."

In 1950, when persecution and torture had become the order of the day, a Chinese superintendent wrote: "We could never have been able to face the attack that came and the persecution, if the Lord had not sent us the revival of the years after 1930. Now, we are able to stand in the evil day. The foundation that was laid then stands sure."

It seems that after Marie left China in 1932, the revival continued, and perhaps even grew in intensity. In Norway, a letter written by a missions' leader in one area came into her hands. Here is what he wrote: "Before the spiritual awakening, our churches were very weak and far too dependent on the mission. We had eight little churches and three Chinese pastors who were almost entirely supported by mission funds. Only six years later, we had forty-four churches, and a large number of them were self-supporting. We then had nineteen pastors wholly or in part supported by the churches. (At the time of the revival) most of our pastors and preachers were truly born again. Before the revival, when we spoke of the (Chinese) leaders and the churches taking over the responsibility for the work, they did not understand us. They shook their heads and said to one another: 'What do the missionaries mean by this? It is completely impossible to expect anything like that of us.' After the revival, we never heard that kind of talk. They began of themselves to do what before was thought impossible."

Although Marie never returned to China, her legacy of uncompromising faith, unquenchable zeal, and the necessity of changed hearts and lives fully committed to the cause of Christ lives on in the Chinese Church today.

The Lord used Marie in His service during her thirty years in her homeland. In her own words, ". . . after groping about for a while like an ordinary missionary on furlough, I was given just what I needed, when the Lord appointed me to service behind the front lines in our own country. This meant starting again from the beginning in prayer for a revival that was a work of the Spirit, just as we had done in China. Besides this, my God-appointed work was among believers who did not seem to have strength enough "to stand in the evil day." It was like life-saving work, throwing out the lifebuoys of the Word to sinking souls who felt they were going under in the storm. Countless S.O.S. calls came from people, mostly unknown to me personally." She counted over 2,000 of these S.O.S. calls in just one year. The Lord also lay on people's hearts to send her postal stamps that made her marvelous "mail ministry" possible.

Part Two: A Vision is Formed

Marie later in Norway.

Sometimes missionaries are well-known in the homeland, but little known in the land of their foreign service. This proved to be the opposite with Marie Monsen. In 1999, a Chinese house church leader, Brother Yun, happened to be speaking in the city of Bergen, Norway. His hosts asked him if he would like to visit the grave of Marie Monsen. Yun was excited to have a chance to thank God on behalf of Henan's Christians for the blessing this small woman had been to them. They walked around the graveyard for a few minutes, hoping to see her name on one of several hundred tombstones. Not being able to locate Marie's grave, they went to the office for help. After flicking through records, the graveyard administrator told them, "Marie Monsen was indeed buried here in 1962. But her grave was left untended for many years, so today it is just an empty lot with no headstone."

Yun couldn't understand how a woman so loved and respected thousands of miles away in China be treated so shamefully in her hometown? Brother Yun said, "In Chinese culture, the memory of people who did great things is cherished for generations to come, so I never imagined that such a thing could happen. The local believers explained that Marie Monsen was still held in high regard and that they had honored her memory in different ways, such as the publication of her biography decades after she had died. But to me her unmarked grave was an insult that had to be made right."

With a heavy heart, Brother Yun sternly told the Norwegian Christians, "You must honor this woman of God! I will give you two years to construct a new grave and headstone in memory of Marie Monsen. If you fail to do this, I will personally arrange for some Christian brothers to walk all the way from China to Norway to build one!

Part Two: A Vision is Formed

"Many brothers in China are skilled stonecutters because of their years in prison camps for the sake of the Gospel. If you don't care enough, they will be more than willing to do it!'

On September 1, 2001, exactly 100 years to the day since Marie Monsen had first arrived in China, more than 200 Norwegian Christians gathered at the graveyard in Bergen. They held a memorial service and thanked God for the life of Marie Monsen. They also unveiled a new memorial headstone.

Marie Monsen never married and had no children of her own. However my daughter, Gloria, as she searched the Internet for information on the life of Marie, came up with the following interesting observation:

My husband's parents named him with the same initials as his uncle (Marie Monsen's brother-in-law) with the hopes that he would someday be his great-uncle's heir, since the C. M. Stendals were childless. The material riches never came to our side of the family, but there was also a spiritual legacy. The Lord must have chuckled as he gave Chad's mother what she asked for, just not what she had imagined.

We are told that the overriding theme of Marie's preaching was *repentance toward God, and faith toward our Lord Jesus Christ.* One hundred years later, the overriding theme of my husband, Chad's preaching has been *repentance toward God, and faith toward our Lord Jesus Christ.*

During the years 1927-1932, Marie Monsen was in China in places where she was the only foreign missionary, during the beginning of the communist guerrilla uprising. Marie was held captive by pirates for 23 days in 1929. Our son, Russell, was held captive for 142 days in 1983. Now, many years later, Russell is dealing with the same guerrilla spirit of communism here in Colombia in places where he is the only foreign missionary. China fell prey to it; we hope and pray that Colombia will not.

Bibliography

Monsen, Marie, *The Awakening, Revival in China 1927—1937,* Strategic Press, Elkhart, IN www.LivingFaithBooks.com

Monsen, Marie, *A Present Help, 1960,* (later published under the title Wall of Fire, Bethany House Publishers, Minneapolis, MN 1967)

Carlberg, Gustav, *China in Revival* pp. 67-83, 1936.

Crawford, Mary K, *The Shantung Revival,* 1933.

Culpepper, C.L., *The Shantung Revival*, 1968.

Pictures:

Page 228: Book Cover; *Marie Monsen,* by Olaf Golf

Page 230: Graciously granted by Sharla Matthews

Pages 243 and 254: http://www.nrk.no/programmer/radio/mellom_himmel_og_jord/1482147.html

Page 255: Book Cover; *Living Water,* by Brother Yun

Afterward

Yes, we did get to Colombia, but not before the Lord took us through a lot of interesting experiences. The next part of our lives, linguistic training, jungle camp in Mexico, and our first year in Colombia will be told in my next volume *Minnesota Mom III* – "The Making of a Missionary."

All 4 of our children grew up in Colombia.

Our sons, Russell and Chaddy both married Colombian women. After Russell was kidnapped in 1983, and the Lord used Chaddy to secure his release, the Lord has used them to raise up a ministry to the war-torn part of eastern Colombia. Currently nine radio transmitters are broadcasting the Gospel in many different parts of Colombia, but especially the eastern plains area.

Our daughter Sharon became a registered nurse, and she and her husband, Bob Jackson, worked with us in ministering to the Kogi tribe for ten years after their marriage. They are now involved in other ministry in the USA.

Our daughter, Gloria, had not yet been born in the time spanned by this present volume. She and her sons have become very involved with the Kogi tribe, the people group to whom we were eventually sent. She grew up with these people and feels like a sister to them, and they also esteem her greatly.

Now some of our grandchildren are becoming involved, so this has become a three-generational, on-going ministry. All 15 of our grandchildren are bilingual, bicultural, dual citizens.

I could never have imagined back in the '50's and '60's as I struggled through the experiences here related, that God had such a wide-reaching plan for us in Colombia, but it all hinged on my obedience.

As you commit your life unreservedly to Him, and hear the voice of the Good Shepherd leading you on, only eternity will reveal the fruition of God's plans for you and your family.

Books in this series written by
Patricia Carlson Stendal

Minnesota Mom in the Land of the Ancient Mother

Volume 1: Beginnings — Long Ago and Far Away

Volume 2: A Vision Is Formed — Pat's Life in Minnesota

Volume 3: The Making of a Missionary — SIL, Jungle Camp and 1st year in Colombia

Volume 4: A Vision is Realized — Living with Santiago, etc. thru 1st Furlough

Volume 5: Christ Lives in Weakness -- Living in Mamarongo — 1969 thru 1978.

Volume 6: Sons Are Rising Up That Are Not of the Mother.

For more information: patstendal@aol.com

Website: www.colombiaparacristo.com

Books written by the Stendal Family

High Adventure in Colombia
    by Chad Stendal

The Guerrillas Have Taken Our Son
    by Chad & Pat Stendal

Walking In The Spirit
    by Chadwick Martin Stendal

40 Years in Colombia
Lomalinda: There and Back Again
    by Patricia & Gloria Stendal

This Gospel of the Kingdom
    by Chad Stendal

Are Millions of Christians Really Safe?
    by Chad Stendal

The Problem Christ Came to Solve
    by Chad Stendal

Rescue The Captors
    by Russell Stendal

The Beatitudes: God's Plan For Battle
    by Russell Stendal

The Tabernacle of David
    by Russell Stendal

The Elijah Who Is To Come
    by Russell Stendal

...And The Earth Shall Respond To The Wheat...
    by Russell Stendal

If you would like to make a contribution and receive a tax-deductible receipt:

In the USA:
Chad & Pat Stendal
Pan America Mission Inc.
P.O. Box 429,
Newberg, Oregon, USA 97132-0429
http://www.panamericamission.org/

If you would like to make a contribution and receive a tax-deductible receipt:

In Canada:
Colombia Para Cristo Society
12629 - 248th St.
Maple Ridge, BC V4R 1K4
CANADA

TO ORDER ANY OF THESE BOOKS

Ordering books in the USA:

Dwight Clough
1223 West Main Street #228
Sun Prairie, WI 53590

books@dwightclough.com
http://www.dwightclough.com/

PARA PEDIR ALGUNO DE ESTOS LIBROS

Librería en Colombia:

Colombia Para Cristo
Calle 44 #13-69 Local 1
Bogotá, Colombia
Tel: (571) 346-1419 * 338-3807

Email: libreria@fuerzadepaz.com
www.fuerzadepaz.com

A Minnnesota Mom

In the Land of the Ancient Mother

VOLUME I
Beginnings

PATRICIA CARLSON STENDAL

Check www.dwightclough.com/Stendal for updates!

Book or booklet	Price	How many	Amount
Rescue the Captors	$10		$
Rescue the Captors 2	$6		$
The Guerrillas Have Taken Our Son	$10		$
Minnesota Mom I	$10		$
Minnesota Mom II	$12		$
Walking in the Spirit in Colombia	$10		$
Are Millions of Christians Really Safe?	$1		$
The Problem Christ Came to Solve	$1		$
The Tabernacle of David	$1		$
The Elijah Who Is To Come	$1		$
This Gospel of the Kingdom	$1		$
Earth Shall Respond to the Wheat	$1		$
Subtotal			$
Priority mail shipping			$ 5.00
Outside USA add $5 per book, $1 per booklet shipping			$
Additional donation to Stendals if desired			$
Total in US Dollars			$

Make your payment to: **Dwight Clough Ministries**

Ship to: Name	
Address	
City	
State/Province	
Zip/Postal/Country	
Email & Phone	

1 *Send your order to*: **Dwight Clough Ministries**
1223 West Main Street #228, Sun Prairie, WI 53590 USA
books@dwightclough.com * Home 608-834-8291 9am-7pm
www.dwightclough.com/Stendal

Notes

Check www.dwightclough.com/Stendal for updates!

Book or booklet	Price	How many	Amount
Rescue the Captors	$10		$
Rescue the Captors 2	$6		$
The Guerrillas Have Taken Our Son	$10		$
Minnesota Mom I	$10		$
Minnesota Mom II	$12		$
Walking in the Spirit in Colombia	$10		$
Are Millions of Christians Really Safe?	$1		$
The Problem Christ Came to Solve	$1		$
The Tabernacle of David	$1		$
The Elijah Who Is To Come	$1		$
This Gospel of the Kingdom	$1		$
Earth Shall Respond to the Wheat	$1		$
		Subtotal	$
		Priority mail shipping	$ 5.00
Outside USA add $5 per book, $1 per booklet shipping			$
		Additional donation to Stendals if desired	$
		Total in US Dollars	$

Make your payment to: **Dwight Clough Ministries**

Ship to: Name	
Address	
City	
State/Province	
Zip/Postal/Country	
Email & Phone	

1<u>Send your order to</u>: **Dwight Clough Ministries**
1223 West Main Street #228, Sun Prairie, WI 53590 USA
books@dwightclough.com * Home 608-834-8291 9am-7pm
www.dwightclough.com/Stendal

Check www.dwightclough.com/Stendal for updates!

Book or booklet	Price	How many	Amount
Rescue the Captors	$10		$
Rescue the Captors 2	$6		$
The Guerrillas Have Taken Our Son	$10		$
Minnesota Mom I	$10		$
Minnesota Mom II	$12		$
Walking in the Spirit in Colombia	$10		$
Are Millions of Christians Really Safe?	$1		$
The Problem Christ Came to Solve	$1		$
The Tabernacle of David	$1		$
The Elijah Who Is To Come	$1		$
This Gospel of the Kingdom	$1		$
Earth Shall Respond to the Wheat	$1		$
Subtotal			$
Priority mail shipping			$ 5.00
Outside USA add $5 per book, $1 per booklet shipping			$
Additional donation to Stendals if desired			$
Total in US Dollars			$

Make your payment to: **Dwight Clough Ministries**

Ship to: Name	
Address	
City	
State/Province	
Zip/Postal/Country	
Email & Phone	

1<u>Send your order to</u>: **Dwight Clough Ministries**
1223 West Main Street #228, Sun Prairie, WI 53590 USA
books@dwightclough.com * Home 608-834-8291 9am-7pm
www.dwightclough.com/Stendal

Notes

Check www.dwightclough.com/Stendal for updates!

Book or booklet	Price	How many	Amount
Rescue the Captors	$10		$
Rescue the Captors 2	$6		$
The Guerrillas Have Taken Our Son	$10		$
Minnesota Mom I	$10		$
Minnesota Mom II	$12		$
Walking in the Spirit in Colombia	$10		$
Are Millions of Christians Really Safe?	$1		$
The Problem Christ Came to Solve	$1		$
The Tabernacle of David	$1		$
The Elijah Who Is To Come	$1		$
This Gospel of the Kingdom	$1		$
Earth Shall Respond to the Wheat	$1		$
Subtotal			$
Priority mail shipping			$ 5.00
Outside USA add $5 per book, $1 per booklet shipping			$
Additional donation to Stendals if desired			$
Total in US Dollars			$

Make your payment to: **Dwight Clough Ministries**

Ship to: Name	
Address	
City	
State/Province	
Zip/Postal/Country	
Email & Phone	

1_Send your order to_: **Dwight Clough Ministries**
1223 West Main Street #228, Sun Prairie, WI 53590 USA
books@dwightclough.com * Home 608-834-8291 9am-7pm
www.dwightclough.com/Stendal

Notes

Check www.dwightclough.com/Stendal for updates!

Book or booklet	Price	How many	Amount
Rescue the Captors	$10		$
Rescue the Captors 2	$6		$
The Guerrillas Have Taken Our Son	$10		$
Minnesota Mom I	$10		$
Minnesota Mom II	$12		$
Walking in the Spirit in Colombia	$10		$
Are Millions of Christians Really Safe?	$1		$
The Problem Christ Came to Solve	$1		$
The Tabernacle of David	$1		$
The Elijah Who Is To Come	$1		$
This Gospel of the Kingdom	$1		$
Earth Shall Respond to the Wheat	$1		$
		Subtotal	$
		Priority mail shipping	$ 5.00
	Outside USA add $5 per book, $1 per booklet shipping		$
	Additional donation to Stendals if desired		$
		Total in US Dollars	$

Make your payment to: **Dwight Clough Ministries**

Ship to: Name	
Address	
City	
State/Province	
Zip/Postal/Country	
Email & Phone	

1*Send your order to*: **Dwight Clough Ministries**
1223 West Main Street #228, Sun Prairie, WI 53590 USA
books@dwightclough.com * Home 608-834-8291 9am-7pm
www.dwightclough.com/Stendal